OUTSIDE THE CAVE

3

GEORGIA S. McDADE

Outside the Cave 3 © 2016 Georgia S. McDade

All rights reserved. No part of this publication may be reproduced or transmitted in any form or by any means, electronic or mechanical, including photocopy, recording, or any information storage and retrieval system now known or to be invented, without permission in writing of the author, except by reviewers who wish to quote brief passages in connection with a review written for publication in print and electronic form.

Cover Art © Adam Korpak

Book & Cover Design by Vladimir Verano, Vertvolta design
www.vertvoltapress.com

Contact the author:
gsmcdade@msn.com

FIRST EDITION

ISBN: 978-0-9821872-1-0

Always hoping a word, a sentence, gesture, or act will help someone, I dedicate *Outside the Cave III* to all of the people who want all of the people unconditionally all of the time and everywhere to be treated as the human beings they are.

ACKNOWLEDGEMENTS

As always, I thank the persons who responded to my writings and took the time to inform me that they like a particular poem or understood "exactly" what I mean. With no readers I would write, but probably never would I have devoted the time I have given the poetry and its publication. Many of the persons in this group are members of the African-American Writers' Alliance and attendees of Writers Read at Seattle Public Library's Columbia City Branch. Participants in both groups have been of particular assistance through their willingness to listen to what I have to say.

I thank all artists and writers whose works served as inspiration for poems in this volume: Holly Ballard Martz, Gordon Nealy, and Chaz Lindsey.

I thank David Preston who read and commented on the draft.

I thank Adam Korpak who read and commented on some of the poems and perennially asked, "When are you publishing the book?" I thank him for designing the cover. Most of all I thank him for more than three decades of stimulating conversations.

I thank my friend Pamela Beatty for writing the foreword in the midst of perhaps the largest upheaval in her life.

Georgia S. McDade, Ph. D.

CONTENTS

(Poems listed in the order they appear in the book.)

FOREWORD i
INTERROGATIVES

    CARE 1
    WHAT AM I TO DO? 1
    FAILING MEMORY 2
    TREES AND FORESTS 3
    A RANDOM MOVE 4
    QUESTIONS FOR GOD 5
    WHY NOT? 6
    HIS FINAL ACT FOR HER 7
    TWO PICTURES 9
    A CHILD AND AN ADULT WATCH TV 10
    COMPLETE 11
    LATE AND FUTURE APOLOGIES 12
    WHERE IS GEORGE BUSH? 14
    AN AMERICAN EXERCISE 15
    EXPLANATIONS 16
    SOMETIMES I CAN'T 20
    SHOOTINGS 21

EXCLAMATIONS

    VALIDATION NEEDS 25
    UNWANTED LOVE 25
    THE FOOTSTEPS 26
    CHARADES AND MASQUERADES 28
    WHERE TO WASH 30
    THE CHANGE 30
    FLASH: BREAKING NEWS 31
    REFUGEES 32
    THE EMPEROR 33
    SPEAKING OF THE EMPEROR 34

| Knowing | 34 |
| Black All of Her Life | 35 |

Imperatives

The Discomfort of Relativity	39
What I Hear	40
Sitting and Standing	41
Suggestions	42
Your Standard	43
What We Want	44
Can't Forget; Forgive	44
Ask Questions Later	45
Justice	46
Grim Reaper	47
News	49
Trust God	51
Little You and Big I	52
Afraid for My Life I	53
Afraid for My Life II	54
Afraid for My Life III	56
Accepted Silences	57
Mr. Right	58
Six and Sixty	59
Occupy	60
Re-Register with the Rabbi	62
Non-Fiction Please	63
Losses	64
Uppermost	65
Stuck	66
Do Better	67
Preparing for Christmas	68

Declarations

Cry	73
Somebody	74
Your Pool	75

Repercussions	76
Loving Couples	77
The Throw-Away People	78
Merging of Mom and Me	79
Being Myself	82
Nothing Goes Away	83
Emmett Till—Again	84
Aware	86
Benefits of Reading	87
Past, Present, and Future	88
Not Having Your Way	89
The Need for Money	91
Puzzle Solved	92
Trauma	93
My Mantra	94
Responses	95
Diversity	96
Wondering vs. Knowing	98
In an Instant	99
His Ways	101
Why They Don't Tell	102
Michelangelo	103
Kudos to the Pope	103
The Value of a Study	104
Disadvantages Overcome	105
Residents	106
Understanding	108
No Thing	109
The Feeling of Fatigue	110
Filtering	112
Teeth	113
Confronting Racists	114
A Way	115
Real Peace	116
The Best Teachers	118
Where I Sit and Stand	119
What Some Mothers Teach	120
The Haul	120

In the Same Situation	121
The Stress	122
Head, Heart, Gut	123
Heaven	124
Hell	126
One Day	127
Confessions	129
A Brief History	130
My Craziness	132
A Mind of Its Own	133
Silent Dolls	135
The Deed	137
Two of Me	138
"Obama Wins"	139
Why We Fall in Love	143
A Family	144
Staying	144
Waiting	145
Selling	147
Definitely Ill	148
My America	149
What Was Taken	152
My Friends	153
Plagues	154
Half Lies, Partial Truths?	155
Half the World	156
Police Action	157
Views from an Axe and a Tree	158
A New Revelation	159
Good Tireds	160
Perils of Their Way	161
Police at Work	162
Thankful	163

Foreword

GEORGIA STEWART MCDADE'S COMMAND OF ENGLISH as well as the span of subjects she speaks to in her poetry makes reading her work both intriguing and edifying and even personal. She speaks of family matters and relationships. She touches on today's politics and asks questions of tomorrow. She is funny at times, deeply moving at times, and always thought provoking.

Her poetry appeals to a broad audience. Each reader is bound to find something that moves, touches, or makes him/her laugh out loud. In "Loss of Memory," for example, Georgia humorously describes the challenges of short-term memory in our later years. In her poem "The Need for Money" she argues against the "money is the root of all evil" theory and adds another perspective. She champions the education and safe keeping of children. She shares personal perspectives on being afraid and wanting to feel safe. She champions being uniquely herself in "Puzzle Solved": "I believe my brother when he says, "There's nothing wrong with being a puzzle as long as there are no pieces missing." She asks us to reflect on those who are refugees in other countries:

"How many people can't sing in a foreign land?

What has the world lost because these people could not sing their songs?"

Some of Georgia's poems take us deeper into ourselves where we have to find our own answers. In "His Final Act for Her" she questions motives and past behavior. In "Questions for God" Georgia asks the questions so many of us ask when tragedy strikes. In "One Day" she accepts responsibility for her own part in making this a better world: "I have but patiently to continue my journey, willingly, regularly pointing out the asininity of the past and how today we have to do better, be better, or, at the least, I myself have to do and be better."

She writes about her Southern upbringing and the continuing impact it has on her daily life "up North" and elsewhere. But one can always find hope whether in spite of the antipathy for the first African-American president she describes in "Obama Wins" or when in "My America" she says, "My America has a split personality." Still Georgia has a deep love of life, learning, and freedom. She is simply a voice calling us to think and act at a higher level for the good of others and ourselves.

Pamela Beatty

INTERROGATIVES

Care

One can say, "I care" but not care.
One can care and not say I care.
People do both all the time.
What the world needs is more caring people.
And the world needs them now.
The young, middle-aged, and old need help—
a little help, a lot of help, all kinds of help.
The world needs help.

Won't you care?

10/31/13

What Am I to Do?

What am I to do?
Quick!
Somebody tell me.
Please.
What am I to do?
Do I wait or be still?
Do I ask or seek or knock?
All I seem to remember is fret not.
And I repeatedly fail not to fret.

11/10/12

Failing Memory

Called hundreds of times, the number is 98, not 89!
And the problem is not dyslexia.
But it takes weeks to remember the correct number.

Used scores of times, the honey loquat is taken at the first sign
    of a cold, not the eighth day.
But it takes eight days to remember the loquat.

Acknowledged decades, birthdays and anniversaries
    now pass unnoticed.
But come two, three days, a week later and a belated e-mail,
    call, or card is on its way.

The cable for the camera?

The library book?

Two favorite cassettes?

Call returned? Bill mailed?

Unknown are the whereabouts of all of the above.

Known is the absence of a remedy to eliminate the problems.

In the meantime, the memory goes on, goes down.

How long will it take the failing memory to fail completely,
    remembering only that it remembers nothing?

11/7/13

Trees and Forests

So, the white supremacist wanted Jews dead.

He went to a Jewish Community Center and killed two Presbyterians.

He went to a Jewish retirement home and killed a Catholic.

Amazingly, the seventy-three-year-old KKK member could not tell the difference between the Christians and Jews.

Amazingly, here in the 21st Century the former grand dragon doesn't know many of one religion have friends, real, genuine, honest-to-goodness friends of other religions or no religion.

Jewish, Catholic, Baptist, Buddhist, Sikh, Muslim, Asian, Hispanic, Latino, black, white: any of us could be friends of any in the group.

So many of us look alike.

Sadly, too many of us see a forest but not the tree, see no humans nor behave in a human fashion.

Has anyone spoken to the murderer? Explained his "error"?

Does he have any regrets? Or is the regret only that the dead are not Jews?

Does he see the ignorance?

Does he understand the pain, the loss his ignorance has caused?

Are there others out there who change their ways because they've learned from his ignorance?

04/25/14

A Random Move

Why didn't the bullet hit a tree, a wall?

Why didn't the bullet hit the street, a fence, anything but the man?
This murder was random.
The shooter is probably sorry.
He never meant to hurt this man.
The shooter's target was another man.
The dead man is not the intended target, never was.
He was not the target says the regretful shooter.

Surely that makes a difference to the dead man's parents, wife, and
        kids, and all of those friends, neighbors, and co-workers.

It makes no difference to me.
The shooter's being sorry erases none of the hurt and loss.
Why doesn't a would-be-shooter think of the consequences of his
        actions?
Why doesn't he wonder about his being the object of someone's
        bullet?
How would his mom, dad, sister, brother, cousin, friend feel?
Why do I wonder?

05/26/12

Questions for God

Did God know when the woman selected the granite that falling on
>said granite years later would be the beginning of her end?

Did God know when parents installed the zip line and
>required their son to wear the helmet said items would be instrumental in his death?

Did God know when the child received that gift of a bike, scooter,
>dirt bike, or car it would play a role in the death of that child?

Did God know when the baby was conceived mother would die in
>delivery?

Did God know before the young man took that first flying lesson—
>against his mother's wishes—death would come in the form of a plane crash?

Did God know when the young men entered the city they would
>depart dead?

Did God know when the mother told her son to whistle to abate his
>stuttering the whistling would get him killed?

There are many more questions.

I tell myself I could manage better if I had answers.

I know faith is supposed to answer my questions.

Still, there are times when I feel certain if I could only have an
>answer I could manage better.

Not always patiently but always faithfully wait I for the answers.

08/12

Why Not?

George Bernard Shaw: some men see things as they are and say why; I dream things that never were and say why not.

What if those who decreed the state of Israel but ignored Palestine
    had instead decreed two states?
What if more persons earlier had heeded Rachel Carson?
What if the Supreme Court had not said George W. Bush should be
    president?
What if Al Gore had fought?
What if the Supreme Court had said no to Citizens United?
What if the Court had seen (admitted?) what so many citizens
    saw—legislators could be bought and now, with their ruling, more easily
    and more often bought?
What if the Affordable Healthcare Act had been approved shortly after presented
    and Congress moved to other business of the country?
What if whistleblowers had blown louder, to different people,
    earlier and gotten responses immediately?

Why not do what needs to be done when it needs to be done?
If we see error and have the power to correct error, why can't
    we?
Why can't we alert someone who can correct the error?
Why don't we correct the error as soon as it is discovered?
The longer we put off doing good, doing right, the more
    opportunity harm is afforded.
The better the greater number is treated, the better a greater
    number is served.
The more served better, the better more are served.
Why not?

2012

His Final Act for Her

Awakened by the lack of air, she sat on the bed gasping.
When breath finally came, she haltingly said to her husband in the
      other room she had to go to the hospital.
Roused from his sleep, he hesitated.
But the urgency convinced him he had to act—after he warmed up
      the car.
So the car got warmer; she breathed harder.
Finally, they left.
Only the two of them were en route to the hospital.
Did she talk?
Did he talk?
What did they say?
Was he cursing as he usually did?
Was she pleading as she usually did?
At least they were heading to the hospital.
How could he have known how ill she was?
Did it matter?
What made him bypass one hospital, two miles away?
Was he thinking of the history of segregation?
Was it habit?
Was money on his mind, the cost prohibitive?
Whatever the reason, he drove, drove to the hospital five miles
      away. (Is it only five miles!)

When did her breathing stop?
Did he notice?
What were her last words?
 Had he heard them?

Arriving at the emergency door, he got out of the car, went around to open the car door.

She fell out, dead.

Children, stunned and hurt or hurt and stunned, remained to nurse their questions forever, silently and loudly, between and among each other.

5/26/13

Two Pictures

Sent me a 30 year-old picture
I remember the location
Remember it well
Sitting in a hot sauna
After emerging from the cold Black Sea
Hip, thigh, leg, and foot exposed
Beautiful, smooth.

Sitting in a sauna 30 years later
After emerging from a community swimming pool
Hip, thigh, leg, and foot exposed

Why would the body's owner want to see that long
       forgotten picture?

06/02/15

A Child and an Adult Watch TV

"Why are they siccing the dogs on the people?
Why are the water hoses turned on the people?" asked
    the child.

The people want to vote, said the adult.

"No, said the child, I mean why are the dogs trying to
    bite the people?
Why are the police spraying them, knocking them down
    with the water?"

The people want to vote, said the adult.

"The people will certainly be wet. They may be bitten,"
    said the child.
And what the people want to do is vote?" said the child.

Yes, said the adult.
"But isn't voting a right? Aren't all citizens supposed to
    vote?" asked the child.
That's right, baby. Voting is the right of a citizen.
Yes, you are right.
"Then I don't understand," said the child.
"Neither do I," said the adult. "Neither do I."

12/08/14

Complete

Michelangelo.
See, perhaps he wasn't so different from the rest of us—in
      preparation and inspiration.

Unfinished, some say of some of his sculptures.
As finished as Michelangelo wanted a piece to be, others
      say.
What about as finished as he is?
Why can't the sculpture be a symbolic replica of what
      Michelangelo, all of us human beings are?

Human beings dressed in all of our frailties plus
      limited Time, cramped Space, unmet Needs, squashed Desires:
      Who's to say this "incompleteness" is not
      our best and most accurate depiction? Who's to say we humans are
      not always emerging, only to stop or be stopped in the midst of a
      dream, masterpiece, or life?

04/27/09

Late and Future Apologies

Some New York City Council members, as well as some statesmen, have apologized for their city's/state's "role in sustaining and benefiting from the slave trade," expressing "profound regret for slavery and historic wrongs rooted in racial and cultural bias."

The U. S. Senate in 2001 passed a resolution apologizing to the victims of lynching and their descendants. The British government offered "sincere regrets" over colonial abuses for torturing Kenyans and agreed to pay $30 million dollars in reparation, making this the first time Britain has admitted guilt over colonial-era abuses anywhere ever—50 years later.

Hillary Clinton apologized in 2008 for the federal government's response in the aftermath of Hurricane Katrina of 2005.

It took thirty-seven years for Exodus International* to admit, "We've hurt people" and inflicted "years of undue suffering."

A Seattle mayor apologized to the Chinese for mistreatment.

Such historical apologies tell me one day Supreme Court Justice Antonin Scalia or someone will apologize for what the Justice called "perpetuation of racial entitlement."

One day someone in the Republican Party will apologize for stymying the American government and thus the people as Congresspersons thwarted every move of President Barack Obama.

History is strewn with apologies, but no apology can change the past.
When will people learn that maltreatment at anytime does not eventually become good treatment?

When will people know hurt today cannot be eradicated by an apology decades later, an apology usually not to the victim whose circumstances are not altered?

*Exodus International in 1976 began helping homosexuals who wished to limit their homosexual desires. In 2013 the ex-gay Christian group ended its program and apologized.

06/22/13

Where Is George Bush?

I never thought I would ask "Where is George Bush?"
I never thought I would think about his cronies Cheney, Rumsfeld,
 Ashcroft, and the like. But here I am wondering what in the
 world are they doing.

Here I am with my questions, and I do not have to see an armless
 or legless veteran or another coffin for questions to arise.

Is the six-decades plus President visiting his mom?

Or is he visiting with his dad?

Is he giving an address and being paid more than the year's wages
 per month or the lost pensions of so many?

Is he playing tennis or golf?

Is he in a tavern?

Is he out with his Halliburton buddies?

Is he writing a book?

Is he visiting his kids, grandkid?

Is he in the midst of yet another business deal?

Considering he is someone who never thinks about me, I spend a lot of time
 thinking about him and the havoc he and his supporters and
 my representatives have wreaked on the world, havoc that will be with
 the country long after he is no more.

I wish I didn't.

12/06/12

Explanations

Maybe we never owe anyone an explanation,
    maybe.
But some explanations could possibly solve
    some problems, possibly.
Perhaps some explanations could remove doubt,
    perhaps.

Less than a minute of thinking reminds me that
    explanations can be a slippery slope.

In a minute, hearers ignore or forget views rather judging the
    person explaining and not always fairly and
    honestly.

In a minute hearers often label explanations
    incomplete, probably a lie, definitely a lie!

A poll would probably show hearers are moved neither way:
    pro or con, most believe what they believed before the
    explanations.

Maybe that explains why some explanations are
    not and never will be forthcoming, why we don't always risk giving
    explanations.

09/28/14

An American Exercise

Stunned
Outraged

Tragedy
Shame, shame, shame

Flags at half-mast
Instant memorials
Flowers galore
Candlelight vigils
Prayers at the site, places of worship
Politicians, President included, so sad, so sorry
Many tears
Important folks visiting the families, loads of condolences
A fund set up, contributions of money in a multitude of manners

Something must be done to stop the horror—but now is not
    the time.

Grieving Time

Somberness
And more often Sympathy, Empathy

Anger

Why?
No answer
No satisfactory answer

Senseless

The meaning/interpretation of the Second Amendment,
    arguments about its meaning, interpretation

More and more calls to join, calls to ban guns

Answers the NRA: Guns don't kill; people do.
    Outlaw guns, and only outlaws will have guns.

Tougher laws would not have prevented this tragedy.

Tougher laws would have prevented this tragedy.

Enforce the laws we have....

News, news, news
Several days of news
Lots of speculation

Get pictures, videos.
Witnesses come forward.

Why?
Authorities on mass killers trotted out
Family and friends interviewed.

The killer—no, alleged killer—is paraded before us,
    if he has not rid the world of himself and his particular
    problems.

The public usually learns he was quiet, polite, helpful,
    incompetent.
He's a reject, a loser, maybe an A student.

Often there's no record of doing wrong,

No signals, no signs, maybe a few, nothing big
Nothing like this expected

Bullied?

Copycat?

Fear of copycats?

Lives ended, lives changed—forever.

And then those of us not directly
        connected move on, some of us a
        bit more carefully, slower but we move on
        nevertheless.
University of Texas
San Ysidro
Columbine
Virginia Tech
Tucson
Mt. Hood
Sandy Hook
(These were the first American incidents to come to my mind.
Which mass shootings come to your mind?)

We moved on after each event.
Maybe there's a gathering at the site on anniversaries.

But generally, most of us move on—again.

Until enough of us demand that assault weapons
> be banned, that getting a gun requires more than filling out a form
> and paying a fee, we'll repeat this exercise.

Isn't there something the sane can do other than hope and pray the
> exercise won't be repeated?

Note: Thus far, hoping has not been very successful.
Hope lasts less than the time required to read this poem.

07/21/12

Sometimes I Can't

Sometimes I can't.

Really.

Sometimes I can't.

I know "can" means "to be able to."

I know I may look as if I'm able to.

I may sound as if I'm able to.

I know some folks believe I can.

Physical and mental skills notwithstanding,

    sometimes I can't.

Despite my godmother's telling me, "Could killed Can't

    a long time ago,"

Despite my telling so many so often, "Yes, you can,"

A lesson I have learned more than once is that sometimes

    I can't.

11/13/15

Shootings

On the military base
At the court house
At the movie
At the mall
At the library
At the church
At the schools: kindergarten – graduate
At the fast-food place
At the office
At the house

Think about how many Americans have died from Ebola.
Think about how many have died from gunfire.

What are we survivors thinking?
Isn't there something we can do?
When do we say, "No more" and act to make it a reality?

11/20/14

EXCLAMATIONS

Validation Needs

One award.
Two awards.
Three awards.
Four.

She went home and wailed for more!

04/24/14

Unwanted Love

No I-love-you-anyway soothes me.
The love I want, crave, and need is not the love in your "I love you anyway."
You cannot wipe me out, and then cap your actions with "I love you anyway."
No doubt you take some comfort from your remark.
But keep your love.
Please.
It harms not helps me.

03/0815

The Footsteps

CRUNCH, CRUNCH, CRUNCH, CRUNCH, CRUNCH....
Forty years later the son can vividly recall
      the tramping as Dad left the house that night.
As usual, the kids weren't to listen to the
      lowered voices of the verbally fighting parents.
And as usual, the kids heard but pretended they
      didn't.
Finally, Dad had said, "I'm leaving" and
      shortly thereafter walked out the door he slammed.

Children can't know marriage is not easy, problems precede the
      children, children rarely cause divorce.

For years the son wondered how a father
      could abandon the mother of his child and his child.
The son could see a child changes the relationship: positively
      and/or negatively, greatly and/or more greatly.
Obviously there are three persons in the house rather than two.
All of the strains before baby become heavier.
And the addition can be so demanding in so
      many ways, unexpected ways.
Chores increase exponentially.
Time is gobbled up.
Schedules disintegrate, must be manipulated
      significantly if not abandoned.
Though some persons try, many do not—
      cannot—adapt to these changes.

No one can know how he or she will respond to
        these changes.
More of everything is required: time, patience, money.

The son grew to understand so much.
But still remembering the sound and pace of the
CRUNCH, CRUNCH, CRUNCH, CRUNCH, CRUNCH….
        some forty years later, he cannot understand how his father
        could have abandoned his mother, his four siblings,
        and him, especially him.

11/30/12

Charades and Masquerades

Wow!
Finally!
I know why some of us so easily get in trouble in
    conversations.
Occasionally we discover, usually by accident, what's behind a
    mask.

For ever so much time and so many
    reasons, the wearer chose/chooses not to
    reveal the true face.
And then we must play charades to
    further understand.
Naturally, the games change; the clues
    are not equally good; the
    information is not equally known.

Are all of us wearing masks?
All of the time?

Are we all playing charades?
All of the time?

How was I to know I was in a
    masquerade playing charades?

And then I learn folks do not always
    wear the same masks, not for the
    same persons, and not at all times!

No wonder relationships may have such a
    difficult time, masquerades AND charades.

Wow!

(Warning: This revelation does not necessarily prevent damage to relationships.)

10/02/13

Where to Wash

"There are three places you need soap on your body," the doctor had said matter-of-factly as he made a circular motion near the right armpit, another to the left armpit and a third about two feet lower in front of his pelvic area.

Well, realized the patient standing in the shower, what the doctor
    said is true for some people in the world.
But some folks in the world need additional stops to the left and
    right of those armpits.
And some folks need to stop before the pelvic stop to take care of
    rolls that won't disappear.
Because the doctor lacked the additional top equipment and would
    most likely never have rolls, the patient decided to keep the
    information secret!

09/23/12

Flash: Breaking News!

We often miss all kinds of good things because we are blinded by age, race, gender, education, wealth, color, religion, creed, or the like: that of the other person or our own. Our prejudices can be our best or worst prisoners.

08/01/12

The Change

She fell for him because of his
        urbanity, elitism, and intelligence.
They were young when the magic
        happened.
Everything was magical, for a while.

Exactly what had been a sanctuary eventually became
        a prison, not overnight, not immediately,
        not always obviously.
Her magical world evolved into something she never imagined.

Forgetting how the magic began, she calmly admitted she
        had to leave because of his
        urbanity, elitism, and intelligence.

04/01/13

Refugees

How many persons over how many centuries have been forced to
    leave their homes?
How many have lived with dreams of returning?
How many have resigned themselves to not returning?
The Cleansing
The Discrimination
Anything that diminishes a being.

How many people can't sing in a foreign land?
What has the world lost because these people could not sing their
    songs?

12/06/12

The Emperor

The emperor has no clothes.
Who knows?
The emperor? His supporters? His enemies?
Some don't, but others do.
Why don't the knowledgeable speak up?
We can guess the emperor, who may or may not know, and
        those who curry his favor or rule him won't speak because
        they do not wish to lose position and favor.
But why do the others not speak up?
Surely all are not ignorant.
Surely all are not blind.
Do they wish to avoid the friction?
Don't they know the price of cleaning up/starting over after the
        emperor will be higher, sometimes exceedingly higher, than
        allowing him to ruin what they had?
Don' they know that sometimes all is lost?
Is it truly always easier to stay in a hell they know than venture
        entering a possible heaven?
Do they ever think about the possibility of a better hell?
Or do they say hell is hell?
Do they say they themselves are not unbearably uncomfortable?
Does it not matter that others are uncomfortable, more
        uncomfortable?
More important, is there no thinking of a possible heaven minus
        this emperor?

12/06/12

Speaking of the Emperor

Of the situation, she said, "The emperor has no
    clothes."
He said, "What's an emperor?"
She thought: so, there's no help here.

12/06/12

Knowing

There are times when you know you know.

But sometimes you share what you know
    and are berated and belittled,
    called too critical or judgmental,
    possibly deservedly so.

But the truth does not change.

Unfortunately, Truth often ignores time and convenience.

So there are times when you know you know and keep what
    you know to yourself.

The rub, of course, is knowing when to speak and when to keep
    quiet!

05/11/12

Black All of Her Life

Black.
Black!
Very light skin—don't you dare say "fair."
Below shoulder-length hair—don't you say "good."
Both descriptions fit her.
At a very early age she got anyone who erred straight: "Black, I'm
        black," she said emphatically.
The teen-ager proclaimed more often, more loudly,
        "I'm black."
She married a black man, had black children.
Divorced late in life
Still making it plain, "I'm black."
Black.
Black!
Died suddenly
Took two days before the divorced husband was located
Given the death certificate, he saw the coroner had written
        for decedent's race, "White."

03/12/15

IMPERATIVES

The Discomfort of Relativity

Relativity is not always comfortable to everyone every time.

Yet a well-meaning person often responds, usually to a catastrophe not his or hers, by saying, "It could have been worse."

No doubt!

"You have cancer in one site—alas, some people have cancer in several sites!"

And the speaker may be, probably is, right.

But please note: KEEP THIS TRUTH TO YOURSELF.

Thank you.

09/05/13

What I Hear

  A sociologist told me LBJ is the worst president, not
        because of Vietnam, but because he was the architect of
        the Great Society, making all of those people think they
        could have the same as she!
An anthropologist told me there's no reason to read non–fiction.
Another anthropologist told me Chihuly's glassmaking is not art.
A historian told me seeing plays is a waste of time.
A number of folks of many skills and abilities told me Shakespeare
        makes no sense.
An excellent student told me Michelangelo is overrated.

If you know me, surely you can see as I make my way I pay
        attention but am sometimes barely, rarely influenced by what some of
        my friends and acquaintances say.
(The key to success may be that you and they do the same!)

12/31/12

Sitting and Standing

"Where you sit is where you stand."
Simple and complex.
Most of all, true.

Now don't be discouraged.
You do not have to remain standing
      where you sit.
You have options.
You may crawl, walk, or run from where
      you stand.
But first you must decide to move away
      from where you sit and stand.

01/21/13

Suggestions

Color your hair.
Don't color your hair!
Don't buy that car!
Lengthen that skirt.
Loosen that dress.
Don't buy so many dirndl skirts.
Stay out of heels that high.
Leave that man/woman alone.
Stay with him/her.
Have a baby!
Don't you have any children.
The list goes on.
People with your interest utmost, they swear, present unasked for advice.
Hear their suggestions.
You have to live with your choices.
Maybe those folks will help; maybe they won't.
Thank them graciously and go about your business.
They could be right, but there's a good chance they are wrong.
Sometimes no advice is needed.
As you go about your business, remember help does not always come in the form of suggestions.

05/26/13

Your Standard

You can set your standard as high as you want and live
>up to it, but you can't make others live up to it.

Corollary: And you can't—or shouldn't—get upset when others
>don't live up to your standard.

Why they don't accept your standard is negligible.

(You don't accept their lower or higher standard.

Maybe you should, they may argue, but it is their standard, not
>your standard.)

Discoveries of any magnitude almost always rest on the vision of
>one or two individuals.

Cries of "You work too hard," "You'll never do it," It can't be
>done," "No one will want/use this," "It won't make money," "It will
>cost too much," "You're crazy," "It's dangerous" have always accompanied
>discoveries.

And the creators, inventors plodded on, despite the
>opposition.

If and when the naysayers and you reap the benefits of such
>standards, neither be surprised nor upset when no one
>pauses to thank you, standard-bearer.

Accordingly, let no one nor no thing other than you lower your
>standard.

(BUT BE PREPARED TO SUFFER THE CONSEQUENCES!)

05/24/13

What We Want

You may sit at home or stand on the corner and wish
    you were
        wealthier
        happier
        healthier
        shorter
        taller
        prettier
        smarter
        etc.

OR, AS M'DEAR SAYS, "TAKE WHAT YOU HAVE AND ARE AND MAKE WHAT YOU WANT."

05/17/13

Can't Forget; Forgive

We will not forget, says Iran.
We will not forget, says Israel.
We will not forget, says the US.

So, not forgetting has not ended the problem.
Perhaps we should select another action.
What about "forgive"?
Perhaps we who won't forget should forgive.

04/30/15

Ask Questions Later

Broken tail light
Loose cigarettes
A box of cigars
Walking down the street blocking traffic
Whistling
Voting
Helping /transporting folks to vote

What above can get you killed?
All of the above.
All of the above.

In the United States of America, all of the above can get an individual killed. Ask survivors of the guilty parties.

04/12/15

Justice

I want justice.
We want justice.

If anyone has any information....
Please turn yourself in....
I want justice....
The injured person pleads for justice.
Survivors beg for justice.

What will "justice" do?
Not one injury will be healed or healed
 more rapidly.
No one will get up from the grave.
The pain remains.

What happens if they don't get
 justice?

Give them justice.
Maybe they know something I do not
 know.

03/22/13

Grim Reaper

Fast or slow

Always near

Often uncomfortably near

Usually unknown and unseen

Will Grim Reaper collect as the result of a fall—in a house or on a mountain? Immaterial.

Will Grim Reaper capture one as the result of a crash—car, bus, plane, bike, or jet ski?

The fault of the deceased or another?

Friend, foe, or neither?

A bullet for the institution, demolition, or preservation of a specific brand of democracy?

A bullet accidentally or randomly loosed by friend, foe, or neither?

Is the site with the military, on the street, or in the home?

Intended or not?

Is the weapon a gun or knife, a coffee cup or baseball bat?

Did someone hit someone too hard or hard enough?

Will it come via food—something we liked or disliked? Choking perhaps?

Will it be medicine—prescribed or not?

At the hands of one who heals or hurts?

Or will it be one of those 1000 ways to die?

Young, old, in-between?

In the womb or soon after emerging?

In the prime of life—whatever that is? A Methuselah?

Immediately before or soon after the realization of a life-long dream? On top of the world? In the pits?

The GR rules eventually, if not today then tomorrow or the next day.

The best preparation is not putting off what's valued—if it hurts no one, yourself included, act.

08/23/12

News

Extra! Extra! Read all about it!
White people are calling racist acts racism!
Repeat: White people are calling racist acts racism.
The 21st Century.
Attention will be paid now.
Not immediately, of course.
But the march is underway.
Not four centuries ago when white
        indentured servants had a date for the
        end of their servitude
Not over two centuries ago when the
        Declaration and Constitution
        were ratified
Not more than a century ago when the Dred
        Scott Decision was decreed, the 13th, 14th, and 15th
        Amendments ratified
Not Plessy vs. Ferguson
Not Brown vs. Board of Education
Not the Civil Rights Bills of 1964 and '65

Not one of the above had the populace say
        racism must be routed or, at least, not
        enough people said it or said it loudly enough.

Now, with the first black President—one in 44—more and
        more whites are calling racism racism.

And some of us can be happy because of the
> realization by so many yet always aware
> that the silence has done irreparable harm, harm that will
> sometimes flare but forever haunt.

Extra. Extra. Read all about it.

10/10/15

Trust God

Unsuccessful business?
Trust God.

Failed marriage?
Trust God.

Sick mother?
Trust God.

Lost child?
Trust God.

Whatever the matter.
Trust God.

Often great advice from the problem-free somehow dwindles or disappears when the problem-free becomes the problem-laden.

Blessed is the one whose Trust God mantra changes not.

03/08/15

Little You and Big I

"Little man in a big position." said the preacher.
"Therein lies the problem!"
"Amen!" said the listeners all over the place.

Now another problem: not one person concluded, "I'm a
    little person in a big position; I should step down."
All fingers pointed toward others: you are the problem; I
    am not the problem.
So we can expect the problem to go on for a while....

03/27/15

Afraid for My Life, Part I

Afraid for my life.
I don't doubt a person who says, "I'm [was] afraid for my life."
But I sometimes ask why the fear.
Did the feared person do something?
Say something?
Hear something?
See something?
Touch something?

Was something done to this feared person?

Why be afraid?

Was what makes the survivor fear possibly the same fear in the
        dead?

Police almost always say they feared for their lives after they have
        shot a person, the unarmed and/or mentally ill, young and
        old included.
Does anyone count how often the dead suspect was unarmed?
How often were the victims mentally ill?
Did the victims harm the wrong person, a person not guilty?
How many of the dead are dead because they feared for their
        lives — had good reasons to fear and should have feared for
        their lives?
Of course, their physical lives!
But what of their mental, emotional, economical lives?
What of their medical lives?

What role did these lives play in the killed's arriving at this point?
Most, if not all, of these questions go unanswered.
Speculation usually rules here.
Accuracy is often on holiday.
No one may speak for the killed, but the possibility exists that the
    killed may indeed have rightly feared for their lives.

07/20/13

Afraid for My Life, Part II

Zimmerman feared for his life.
But when did he become afraid for his life?
Obviously not when he volunteered for such a task
    nor when he called the police over 200 times.
Was it when he got his gun?
Was it the minute he saw the young man he was following?
Was it when he saw the young man was black?
Did he see black first?
Did he see anything after seeing black?
Were black and male ever separate?
Was there no thought of human being?
Of young man?
Of someone's son, brother, father, or friend?

Did he become afraid for his life when the dispatcher told him to
    stay in his car?
Did he become afraid when he got out of his car?
Did he become afraid when he realized he could be beaten?

There are so many questions.
Well, all questions except was he afraid for his life are irrelevant
    says the just judge, the justice-seeking judge.
Instructions were given.
There is no space to ask if the dead feared for his life.
There is no space to ask the dead if he believed he was the
    murderer's prey.
The perpetrator feared for his life, so the verdict had to be as it is.

07/20/13

A lawyer friend says nothing was wrong with the judge's instructions; they were good. The flaw was with the juror who, after the trial, said, "He got away with murder." It was up to the juror not to be swayed. But, says the lawyer, the person selected foreperson is usually the most articulate and/or the socially highest ranking person on the jury. A person who feels inferior is not going to disagree with the foreperson.

08/11/13

Afraid for My Life, Part III

I fear for my life.
I have yet to get a gun.
I'm always glad I was not home when my house was burglarized.

Verdicts such as Zimmerman's make me afraid for my life.
How long have I endured such "justice"?
No, how much longer must I endure it?
With the bogs of limited life and minimal liberty occupying so much of my time and energy, will I ever get to pursue happiness?

I am afraid for my life.
I have a headache.
I breathe heavier.
I am stymied.
I am stultified.

I am among the millions who have waited for the arc to get to justice....
Exactly how long is this arc?

And then another case comes, and I am more afraid.
I can't help wondering if anyone will defend me in my lifetime.
Please give me the courtesy I give you.
Believe me when I say I am afraid for my life.

07/20/13

Acceptable Silences

Some secrets are made to be kept.
Never tell your child, "I do not know who your father is."
Never tell your child, "Mom [Dad] did not want you."
Never tell your child, "You are ugly."
Never tell your child, "You will never amount to anything."
Never tell your child, "You are stupid [dumb]."

There's usually no need to reveal a secret that may indeed relieve you—probably temporarily—but burden another—possibly permanently.

(If you have to tell, tell the therapist.)

05/21/13

Mr. Right

He can dance all night long.
But he can listen too—all night if necessary.
He can talk too, not chatter but converse.
His thinking is unrivaled—be the subject politics or religion.
He knows of what he speaks.
He understands, can disagree or concede with equanimity.
He can tear an argument apart.
He can put an argument together with the same aplomb.
Character fills every aspect of his life.
His integrity is sound.
Like her, he goes just about everywhere, anywhere she wants to
    go, willing to try the new and revisit the old.
His generosity knows no bounds.
His constancy is calming, his love genuine.
His education the broadest, never overbearing nor inferiority-
    causing.
He holds her interest as she does his.
He's passionate though not out of control.
He's healthy in every way: mentally, emotionally, physically,
    financially, and spiritually.
To top it off, he's at the helm of good humor.
He's always dressed well and appropriately.
Now, she always envisions him clearly.
Her one request of you: please direct him her way!

01/11

Six and Sixty

Better to be told you're cute at six than sixty!

Don't misunderstand.
Being on the receiving end of this statement is good at any age.

But at sixty, we generally know we are or aren't all kinds of
        things.
Generally, we have learned to take or leave comments.
Generally, we know when folks are telling us the truth or lying.
And most importantly, we go about our business despite what
        one says or doesn't say.

But, God willing, a six-year-old has a long way to go.
Being told she is cute can be helpful.
The kid who always breaks spirits—seems each class has at
        least one such fellow—is not as successful if the little girl
        has been told at home she is cute.
And how cute she is does not matter.
What matters is who says it.

Many are the girl and boy significantly slowed because a mom
        or dad commented negatively about a feature over which
        the little listener has no control.

So, tell them they're cute.
But please, please don't wait until they're sixty!

08/14/13

Occupy

Request, command: Occupy. Occupy!
Of course, occupy the banks.
But also occupy government—local, state, and
    national.
Occupy legislative, judicial, and executive branches.
Occupy the police forces all over the
    the world.
Occupy military complexes everywhere.
Occupy corporations, especially the
    ones that make billions and pay no taxes. (Watch them tell us
    how much they contribute to the community.)
Occupy the religious groups of every kind.
Occupy schools, nursery, k-12, colleges and
    universities, profit and non-profit, vocational, technical, and
    business.
Occupy the unions.
Occupy the contractors.
Occupy the realtors.
Occupy the film industry.
Occupy the music industry.
Occupy the housing industry.
Occupy the telecommunication industry.
Occupy the medical profession.
Occupy the insurance companies—health, house, and auto.
Occupy the pharmaceutical companies.
Occupy the media—newspapers, magazines, radio, and television.
Occupy cable. Please.

And why should so much be occupied,
> you might say.

Simple.

Too many leaders never knew, have
> forgotten, or ignore
> the admirable goals and purposes
> of some founders.

Too many leaders never knew, have
> forgotten, or ignore the morals of those founders.

In almost every instance, the public
> served are the public fleeced.

Rarest are the ones who stand up for
> the least, consider the need rather
> than the want.

Too many are concerned with getting
> more for themselves instead of considering the
> interests of those they represent or serve.

Gandhi was right—again: truth must
> go further than an individual or
> two; truth must spread, and spread
> not only locally or even nationally;
> truth must spread globally. And at
> the bottom of truth is treating everyone, regardless of social
> location, as we wish to be treated.

06/12

Re-Register with The Rabbi
(For only those who consider themselves Christians)

When did you accept Jesus as your Savior?
When did you learn what accepting Jesus means?
Do you still have that enthusiasm?
Do you remember making any promises?
Do you remember what you promised?
Do you and your house serve the Lord?
Do you remember the Sabbath Day and keep it holy?
Do you regularly assemble?
Do you exhort others?

More important:
Do you feed the hungry?
Do you provide water for the thirsty?
Do you house the homeless?
Do you clothe the naked?
Do you care for the sick?
Do you visit the imprisoned?

On second thought, and most important and more direct, ask yourself, have you treated others, including the least, as you wish to be treated?
If the answer is no to the questions above, then you must indeed re-register, if not register, with The Rabbi.

05/19/13

Non-Fiction Please

You write your fiction.
You write it well.
I'll read it.
I'll read it well.
I may like it.

But don't tell me to desert non-fiction if only for a little while.
There's no need for imagination now.

There is too much pain.
There is conflict.
There is too much failure.
There is much confusion.
There is crying.
There is too little laughter.
There is strength.
There is success.
There are too many kindnesses.

There is room for both of us.
I'll do my work; you do yours.

06/22/13

Losses

There are times when everybody loses, everybody.
Some of us, however, lose more than others.
Sometimes we know immediately this is the case.
Other times we see it soon, gradually, eventually.
Sometimes we know how much we've lost.
Other times we discover we've lost more than we could have
        imagined.
Sometimes we have done the best we could to alter the outcome.
Other times we realize we could have done more to alter the
        outcome.
All times we know the loss impacts different folks differently.

Sometimes we must admit everyone does not see nor feel the loss.

Regardless, Time does not stop for us to reset, rewind, redo.

All we can do is take the lesson(s) and apply it (them) as often as
        necessary so as to avoid or reduce forthcoming losses....

No! There is at least one other action—we can share the lesson(s).
What people learn from the same event, incident can be ever so
        different.
Sharing lessons may, therefore, lessen future losses as we work for
        the day when all of us—at least more of us—win.

11/11/14

Uppermost

Life goes on.

Scream, whimper, stand, walk.

Sit, sulk, wail, talk.

Punch, jab, kick, rage, run.

Life goes on.

You may do

        some of the above,

        all of the above,

        none of the above,

        any combination of the above.

Add options if necessary.

Just remember: Life goes on.

05/14/14

Stuck

"Clowns to the left of me,
Jokers to the right,
Stuck in the middle with you."

Well, being stuck any place is probably not a good place.
But stuck in the middle with the right someone is better than being stuck in the middle alone.
However, be sure the companion is neither a disguised clown nor phony joker.

05/23/13

Do Better

When you know better, you do better.
Another of those good-sounding statements,
Another statement that ought to be true.

Little observation shows the statement is not
        necessarily true:
Ask some German World War II or Viet Nam
        babies whose fathers are American, British,
        French, Soviet, German.
Ask the victim or survivor of a drunk driver.
Ask the victim of a driving phone user.
Ask the abused child, spouse, or partner.

The information is out there.
Access is free.

Yet far too many folks do indeed know better but for
        one or many reasons fail to do better.
When you know better, you ought to do better.

05/09/15

Preparing for Christmas

For now,
Put aside the Christmas trees,
The ornaments of every kind.
Remove the angels as well as the angel hair.
Get rid of the icicles, the artificial snow, the snowmen, including Frosty.
Eliminate the popcorn and beads.
Don't think of all of the food and drink labeled traditional.
Put aside Dasher and Dancer and the other reindeer.
 Include Rudolph please.
No wreaths, holly, or mistletoe.
Turn off lights.
Blow out candles.
Silence the music, bells, and carols.
Forget the little drummer boy.

For now, zoom in on the Nativity scene.
See the animals: camels, donkey, cow, sheep.
The camels must be tired.
The donkey's probably tired too.
The cow stands still.
The sheep may remind you that one of His names is Lamb of God.

The animals seem to know to revere the Baby.
No noise, none of those animal sounds.
Note the shepherds.
Imagine what they must have thought when they heard the angel saying "Fear
       not, for behold I bring you great tidings of good joy...."

And those wise men, men who had traveled more than two years say some sources, wise men who presented their gifts of the precious metal gold, expensive perfume frankincense, and anointing oil myrrh.

At all costs they had to come.

But their wisdom prevented them from returning home.

Consider Joseph, how he must have loved Mary.

And focus on Mary, the spirit-filled young girl who changed physically and mentally, the young girl bearing the Baby who would bear the sins of the world.

Now focus more, focus laser-like on the Baby.

The Baby is the center.

He is indeed the reason for the season.

You know His story.

You probably know it well, have heard it since you were a little child.

Put the Baby and His story first, uppermost.

Follow the words of the Baby.

Put those words first in your heart.

Put the words into practice—year round.

Then you can indeed have a merry Christmas.

12/12

DECLARATIONS

Cry?

Cry. Cry! Let it out!

Don't cry.
Don't cry out loud.
Don't let them see you crying.

My vote is for crying—if the need arises.
The catharsis may empower you as nothing else will.

I never forget that Jesus wept and He knew He would
    soon raise the dead Lazarus.
If the need arises, yes, cry.

04/17/13

Somebody

Nobody to step in
Nobody to step up
Nobody to stand in
Nobody to stand out
Nobody to speak up
Nobody to speak out
Nobody to sit in
Nobody to sit it out

                                                for me.

Yet I am.
I am here.
Someone must have stepped in and up.
Someone must have stood in and out.
Someone must have spoken in and out.
Someone must have sat in and sat it out.

      My gratitude knows no bounds to that Someone.

04/29/13

Your Pool

I can't swim in the pool of your thoughts.
Oh, I wish I could!
To know what made you do that or why you didn't do that,
Why you said this or didn't say this,
What you really meant, how long you meant it—
Of course, I would love to know!

I admit knowing what's in your thoughts is a terrible invasion
    of your privacy.
And yet, I selfishly and honestly admit my life would definitely
    be easier if I could occasionally swim in the pool of your
    thoughts.

4/21/07   Inspired by the works of Gordon Nealy

Repercussions

Occasionally I find myself in an undesirable place.
And I accept responsibility.
Sometimes I said yes when I should have said no.
Other times I said no when I could've said yes.
Worse, there were times when a "maybe" was the best
        answer—for me.
But I was not alone.
There was one more person affected; there were two or more
        affected.
My answers affected them and me, sometimes for ages,
        sometimes forever.
Repercussions. Repercussions!
As I attempt to keep the peace, maintain order, I have not always selected
        what I believe is the best answer for me.
I have always gone for the greatest good for the greatest
        number, though this choice too has given and can give ME trouble or,
        at least, put me in a place I had rather not be.
I can't imagine life without repercussions.
But I would like to try living such a life.

10/30/14

Loving Couples

The attention they pay—to each other and what each
    values
The conversations they have—to hear, to respect
The understanding they have—to see each other's vision, dream
    and yet know each other's needs
The ways they look—to gauge each other, as if they are the only
    two persons in the world
The games they play—not the psychological games of demeaning, hurting,
    embarrassing each other but child games of racing to turn out the
    light or not drive.
The gifts they give—a wooden tulip because of a love for tulips, a backrub,
    or any of many acts, kindnesses the other appreciates.
The times they know—when no word is needed and a look
    suffices.
The caresses they give—so natural.

They enhance each other's life in many ways.
Closeness in all its varieties counts.
Both are free to be, to be who they are.
Neither asks, requires that the other be more.
There's no need to give more.
Both give their all and give it all the time, none of this 50-50
    stuff.

C A R I N G is written on everything they say and do.
Such unions are rare but extant.
How fortunate to be part of one!

04/14/13

The Throw-Away People

Despite the modern technology and the increased
        population, our society is throwing
        away more people than ever before.
The Throw-away people are of all ages.
Babies found on doorsteps, in alleys,
        left with grandparents and sitters
        interminably;
Children disciplined with suspensions and expulsions;
Teen-agers whose goal is to live past eighteen years old;
Gangbangers who take lives for the fun of taking lives, to see what
        killing feels like, or to protect their turf;
Foster parents seeking money, servants, sex slaves;
Partners cast aside for a slough of reasons;
Seniors in homes away from home where they never feel at home;
Multiple-year friendships ended because of one action or inaction.

Too often we have neither the skill nor patience
        necessary for satisfactory relationships.
Too often the reason behind the origin of the
        relationship, and certainly its breakdown, escapes us.
What we need to remember is the thrown-away, however, do not
        usually thrive and often prey on the society that threw them away.

04/17/13

Merging of Mom and Me

Long before I saw it, those who knew my mother said I look like her.
Now, as a kid, I worked hard to write like her.
I tried my best to read what she read.
My aunt said the adult me was like her—I could do many things at the same time and do all of them well.
But I did not look like her—then, I thought.
Now I see. Now I see.
Early we girls knew we had legs shaped like my mom's—and loved it.
A childhood friend of hers had not seen me in years; he watched through his curtain as I walked across his yard.
He said to his wife: "Whoever that is walks just like Georgia Stewart."
I had never noticed or thought about our walks.
But now I see.
I realized a few years ago that though my stomach is smaller than hers, it is the same shape.
Hair which I wanted to be salt and pepper IF IT HAD TO BE GRAY was rather exactly like hers—gray around my face but black in the back.
There are a few pictures of my mom the young woman; the nephews always say the pictures are of me.
No telling them the photos are not me convinces them otherwise.
They think I am teasing.
Visits home always get, "Child—girl or baby—you sure look like your mom."
I say nothing.
But I can see.
What cinched the validity of these similarities was a moment of my playfully pestering one of my sisters; she said, "Go on with your M'Dear–looking self."
That sealed it.

How my mom knew to name her second of five girls her namesake, I do not know.
But folks who knew her know for a fact I am a lot like her.
I know I'm wearing her face.
It took decades, but now I see.

11/24/10

Mourning Mountain Climbers

I
will mourn
not one more
mountain climber!
I am tired, very tired of mourning climbers.
I am tired of people who bother mountains,
mountains that move for no one, mountains that care not a bit about who
survives nor survivors of those who do not survive.
Merciless mountains they are.
Nanda Devi Unsoeld 1976
The eleven on Rainier in 1981
Marty Hoey on Everest in 1982
Rob Hall and Scott Fischer in 2001
Now add six more....

Check the list of deceased mountain climbers—
these of the varied ability and age, experts and amateurs, male and female,
many countries of origin, all with money—except the Sherpas.
Rainier, Everest, Denali
They climb the mountain because it's there.
They say they have to climb.
Well, so be it.
But I will not mourn.
I will not mourn any more mountain climbers....

06/02/14

Being Myself

"I am what I am, and that's all that I am."
That's easy for Popeye to say!
I too am what I am.
But I do not always show what I am.
Being what I am can get me in or out of trouble, now or later.
Just as hiding what I am can get me in or out of trouble, now or later.
Yet to make or keep friends and acquaintances
to influence people, win the argument, preserve the status quo, and /or my sanity,
myself even, I am not always free to be what I am.
For scores of reasons.
But this does not change what I am!
In this life there are many roles to be played.
Facets of who I am are variously spotlighted.
I do not always get to choose what to show when to whom.
But what shows is me, maybe not my best me or the desired me but me, nevertheless.
I've learned that in many instances what I am can cause problems for others and/or myself.
And I've seen enough Popeye to know he would agree!

05/17/15

Nothing Goes Away

Some deaths never go away.
We try; we try very hard.
But the weight of the loss won't go away.
A change has come; we know that.
But the death won't go away.

Now instead of the somewhat carefree called the norm is the never,
    ever carefree of the new norm.
Doing what we used to do is never the same, may be negative,
    definitely not positive.

Although one memory may be the impetus for a smile, a laugh,
    the next minute a memory, maybe the same memory, is
    the impetus for tears, screaming.
All the words of advice, encouragement meant to soothe do little or
    nothing, but we mourners usually manage to be polite.

Life divided into before the death and after the death.
What we did, when we did it, how we did it reminds us of the loss.
We are grateful, but gratitude did not save the loved one, cannot
    save us.
We are left to mourn all the days of our lives, not all day every
    day, but often when we are in the midst of something not the
    least bit related.
Perhaps you'll be blessed to avoid such pain.

10/02/14

Emmett Till—Again

At my sincerest, I thanked the four non-blacks who had
> written poems about Trayvon Martin, Eric Garner, and
> John T. Williams.

I thanked them for devoting their time and talent to men
> murdered by police, justifiably so said the courts.

I never believed only blacks are concerned about the
> murders, though I often saw little evidence of being
> correct.

I then told the writers I had been writing about Goodman,
> Schwerner, and Cheney and Emmett Till for decades.

I do not know why I can't get them out of my mind.

I wonder if it is because of my age when they were
> murdered.

Or is it their ages?

Was it that photograph of the battered Emmett *Jet* did not
> hesitate to print?

Perhaps it was the look on Emmett's mother's face.

Maybe it was wondering how helpless Emmett's uncle must
> have felt as he begged the two white men not to take
> Emmett away.

Those mug-shot looking photos of the trio of civil
> rights workers in newspapers around the world plagues
> me still.

The murders of Emmett Till and the trio are only two horrors
> that took place more than half a century ago.

Yet, I can get chill bumps from thinking of them.

I've consciously attempted not to write about these events.
I think I have nothing else to say about Emmett Till; I think
    I've said all I can say.
And then something triggers something, and I'm off—or on—
    again.
Though the lady did not have to tell me "Keep writing about
    Emmett Till," I have a feeling I'll be writing about
    Emmett Till the rest of my life because Emmett Till
    continues—uninvited—to show up in my life.
So, here is my last Emmett Till poem—until the next time.

03/14/15

Aware

"You're in pain," said the doctor immediately after entering his
    office. "Why didn't you call me?"

I did.

"No, you didn't."

Yes, I did.

"You did not call me."

Sitting up in the chair, I said, "I did call you!"

He yelled, "Who took that call?"

Reclining again, I sighed thinking about all of the times I have
    been forced to answer the same question with the same words
    to the same person.
And then I thought of all the times I've been labeled an angry black woman as
    someone replied with, "Do you have to yell?" or, my favorite, "Do you
    have to raise your voice?"
Well, yes, sometimes I have to raise my voice to make my point.

Believe me, I long for the day when the listener takes my yes as
    yes and my no as no.

10/02/14

Benefits of Reading

Reading can save you.
Really.
Now, you must read, not merely call words.

Reading can put you in the middle of conflicts and thereby distract you, give you a reprieve, at least momentarily.
You may observe one or many persons battling one person, a few persons or an army.
You can observe one tiny person battling gigantic nature.
You can observe an individual battling opposition within,
sometimes overwhelming it, other times succumbing to it.
Reading can be the experience you'd never literally get.
But reading allows you to witness, learn, travel.
Reading can teach you.
You can learn about places you want to go.
You can learn about places you'd never want to go.
Reading can assist you in your choices.
Select a character: follow.
That character may demonstrate what to do in life
as easily as demonstrate what not to do.
The only cost is time, and reading time can be some of the time best spent!

Reading can deliver you.

11/07/14

Past, Present, and Future

I'm living in the moment.
I know I may not look to be.
But I am.
I'm focusing.
I'm storing memories for the future.
I know this sounds contradictory.
But too, too many times, someone has left me.
And I've had to struggle more than usual because I miss her and
    him, them so much.
When they were present, the brain, the ears, the hand were working
    but not 100%.
I could've, should've zoomed in on them, our conversations, our
    actions.
I could have questioned more.
I could have listened more.
I could have written more.
Quite truthfully, images and memories get me through some days,
    prod me to try harder, be better.
But despite the present vivid images and memories, I want more
    vivid past images, more past vivid memories.
I can have these for the future if I concentrate on the present.
As I said, this may sound contradictory, but I've had great losses,
    losses of bodies, yes, but minds and spirits too.
Because of the past, I'm dodging voids as I live fully in the
    present preparing, storing for the future.

12/11/14

Not Having Your Way

A young man said his mom had to learn she could not always have her way.

"Forgive him for he knows not what he says." I thought but did not say,
Then I laughed—to myself.

An aka for his and many mothers is "Not-Getting-My-Way-So-Child-Can-Get-Child's Way."
I couldn't decide where to begin the list of sacrifices.
And I was thinking only of times I knew this mother had not had her way!
There's no telling what she could say.

But most moms don't say, never reveal what they did nor how often,
never confess what they didn't do nor how often they didn't do,
never say what they want to or didn't want to say.
Many moms defer and eventually cancel dreams.
Most moms never charge.
Hearing of and knowing there are easy pregnancies and difficult pregnancies is quite different from enduring either pregnancy.
Some moms undergo multiple tests, treatments, and surgeries to get pregnant.
Countless moms have given up school, careers to have healthy babies.
Some have gladly or reluctantly succumbed to bedrest as they knew there were pressing demands; forget about what they wanted.
Some have endured moves they despised, remained in relationships and

marriages they knew that did irreparable harm to them.
Some have put themselves in all kinds of danger to protect their unborn and born, sometimes losing their souls and their lives in the process.

Child, if only you knew—and for all manner of reasons no one will tell you, can tell you—how your mom has learned she cannot have her way. And she continues the practice today, wouldn't have it any other way.

02/04/15

The Need for Money

It's not money that's the root of all evil.
It's love of money that is the root of all evil.
The need for money can be the root of evil:
A mother of thirteen sells the virginity of twelve daughters, $200
        each;
A jobless dad, a long-time jobless dad, kills wife, children, self;
A teen-ager sells drugs, gives money to his mom for younger
        siblings.

Until persons responsible for forming this more perfect union,
        establishing justice, insuring domestic tranquility, providing for the
        common defense, promoting the general welfare, and securing the
        blessings of liberty, we will have humans doing the sub-human.

Hope lies in the fact that we can do what needs to be done now
        and, therefore, reduce significantly causes that sometimes
        render humans less than human.

10/25/13

Puzzle Solved

A real puzzle.

Enigmatic.

A piece of work.

All said in derision

ABOUT ME!

There was a time your descriptions were my problem.
There was a time your descriptions cut me to the bone.

But now I know.

All the pieces are here.
All the pieces fit.

I believe my brother when he says, "There's nothing wrong with being a puzzle as long as there are no pieces missing."

09/14/13

Trauma

Time heals all wounds.
Not necessarily.

Time triumphs.
Usually. Maybe.

Time, however, is trumped by trauma.
All the time.

Chronological order is time in a straight line.
Narrative order is time in and out, skipping about
      beginning in the middle or near the end but always with
      a "The End."

Traumatic order, however, does not exist.
Trauma can come and go.
Come early, stay late.
Leave early, come late.
Be a glint or glance one day.
Hover the next day or—decade.
Sharp pain or dull.
Energize or paralyze.
Trauma mocks time.
Like closure, trauma and its end can be a myth.

03/03/15

My Mantra

The art is three identical rectangle boxes, each about a foot
    long.
Inside each box is a burning light bulb.
Written on each box in big red, all capital letters is, "I'M FINE."
I'M FINE. I'M FINE. I'M FINE.
Laughter came when I saw the title of the art: *My Mantra*
    of Lies Up in Lights.

I wish the artist had said, I'm fine and ended with a question
    mark.
I'm fine and ended with an exclamation mark.
But she said, I'm fine and ended with a period.
Then she titled her piece.

But, no, this is her assessment of herself.
At least she knows she's lying.
We have an advantage, probably a slight advantage, with
    ourselves when we lie and know we are lying.
Some of us lie and forget what we're saying is a lie.

I have to tell her I have my mantra on a poster in my
    bathroom, have had it for years.
It is not always a lie! It won't go up in lights.
I mean it's not true every time everywhere for everything.
But lots of times, it's true; more and more it's true.
In big red letters my mantra reads, "Damn, I'm good."

Inspired by the art of Holly Ballard Martz.   *02/27/15*

Responses

Some days we smile at the situation.
Some days we actually laugh.
Some days we cry.
Some days we are so angry, we simply…

On second thought, we do nothing simply, never have
    that opportunity.

Sometimes on rare, very rare occasions, we fight back
    rather than take a deep breath and swallow, never
    guessing our responses will require more
    responses.
Sometimes we are surprised their responses are about
    their perceptions of us rather than our responses.
By the time the others have gotten their words in—and
    they will get them in—we are often beginning to
    wish we had gulped more air and remained silent.

But wide awake, some of us continue to dream of a day
    when we can be who we are and what we are
    without someone taking offense, patronizing,
    or chastising.

We look forward to and work for the day when there
    will be no need to defend our name.
We know that day is coming.
We do not apologize for being tired nor anxious as we
    do whatever is in our power to make that day
    come sooner rather than later.

01/24/14

Diversity

Diversity.

There's race, of course, say some.
Race may show up most often when the term "diversity" enters the conversation.
But race is far from the only kind of diversity.

Consider the following:
    Gender
    Age
    Color
    Disability
    Ability
    National Origin
    Language
    Background
    Culture
    Employment
    Skills
    Talent.

And there's yet more diversity that's not always considered.
Because of the categories listed above, one must admit diversity in experiences.
It follows then that there exists diversity in opinions.

With so much diversity, acknowledged and unacknowledged,
    recognized and unrecognized, the miracle is that humans—
    evil notwithstanding—have accomplished what they have.
And so despite diversity, I still believe in humans and humanity.

10/13

Wondering vs. Knowing

Did you ever wonder why in the world you made a particular decision?
Did you ever wonder what in the world were you thinking?
You know:
> child conceived/not conceived;
> proposal accepted/rejected
> marriage began/ended;
> property bought/sold;
> letter mailed/unmailed;
> check signed/unsigned;
> position accepted/rejected;
> class completed/discontinued.

Did you know the choice was wrong the next minute, hour, day, week, month, or year?
Or did it take years, a decade or more to realize the error?
Did you come to see that it changed your life profoundly?
I just wonder.
Somehow it seems one act in an instant ought not divide our lives into before and after.
It seems.
And yet one act can indeed divide our lives.
I just wonder.
I know there are times when absolutely nothing can redo or remove, eliminate or erase.
There is no rewinding or recycling.
I know.
About this fact I do not wonder.

11/13/14

In an Instant

Fall, 1957

Little Rock

Elizabeth wanted to go to school, a school the
>Supreme Court said she could attend.

Thousands, really millions, did not want Elizabeth to go to
>"their" school.

Elizabeth's flaw?

Elizabeth is black.

Hazel was only one of those persons, one of the persons who
>did not want Elizabeth at her school.

No, Hazel was by no means alone.

That ubiquitous Everybody was against Elizabeth going to that
>School: her family, friends, and community as enraged as she.

Hazel was at the site, heckling with all her might.

See her photo.

Adults of all ages expressed their displeasure.

Why wouldn't the kids do the same, follow their role models?

Snarling face

"Nigger" spouted countless times

"Two, four, six, eight; we don't want to integrate!"

Exactly what was Hazel saying?

One knows only that Hazel had no pleasant words.

Hazel was saying something to hurt Elizabeth, something to
>make it plain Elizabeth was not welcome.

How could Hazel know this would eventually change her
>life? For good? Or, at least, forever?

Fortunately or unfortunately, Will Counts took a photo,
>   a record for eternity but at the time a record for the
>   world, a record that would change both girls'
>   lives forever.

Years would pass before Hazel would say, "One moment
>   shouldn't define a person's life."

And Hazel is right as right as she was wrong that September day in
>   1957.

But so often what's right does not rule, sometimes for a little
>   time, but sometimes for a lifetime.

11/13/14

His Ways

"If this is how *you treat your friends*, no wonder *you have so few!*"
I did not say this!
I didn't.
Saint Teresa Of Avila said this.
In the 1500s!

Can you see why someone would say this?
Can't you?

His ways are not our ways.

10/23/15

Why They Don't Tell

People keep secrets for all manner of reasons.
They feel stupid.
They think people will think they are stupid.
They are afraid.
They should have known better.
They think people will think they should have known better.
They don't think people care.
They think some people will say, "Good for her!"
They think some people will call them liars.
They think some people will ignore them.
They are embarrassed.
They will hurt other people.
They don't want to be snitches.
They should have run.
They could have run.
They could have just said no.
They think they will be ignored.

People keep secrets for all manner of reasons.
However long it takes people to speak, they should be listened to whenever they speak.
The amount of time it takes for a secret to be revealed does not diminish or eradicate the truth of the secret.

03/17/15

Michelangelo

Obedient, gifted
Reading, interpreting, imagining,
Bible, pigment, walls, windows
Measuring, drawing, painting
Beautiful, sacred
Sistine Chapel.

Kudos to the Pope!

Thank God for the pope, at least Pope Sixtus!
Michelangelo never volunteered to paint the Sistine
        Chapel.
Saw himself as sculptor not a painter,
Following orders, obeying orders.

Sometimes there are advantages to following orders, obeying
        orders—to others and possibly to the obedient one.
The pope had the power.
Thank God for the pope.

10/09

The Value of a Study

Michelangelo would've had an answer for all those folks
    who label some of his works incomplete.
Maybe all he wanted was a study.
Maybe he believed a study was the way to get to
    perfection.
Maybe he knew when we produce without study we
    may indeed have only a product.
He, of course, wanted a masterpiece.
He went through the steps: a thought, a drawing, a
    draft, a scale model, maybe several models.
Finally he took chisel to stone and created sculptures
    that live in the humanities of cultures worldwide and
    centuries later continue to stop both the uneducated and the
    educated in their tracks.

10/01/09

Disadvantages Overcome

When you see your first movie at seventy rather than seven…
When you see your first play, opera, ballet at sixty
>rather than six…
When you see your first Van Gogh at ninety rather than
>nine…
When you take your first plane ride at forty rather
>than four…
When you escape the boundaries of your birth
>country at fifty-five rather than five…

Of course the younger viewer has the opportunity to make
>tremendous gains as a result of such experiences at an early
>age; life may take a completely different course.

But the disadvantage of not having such experiences early is a
>disadvantage that can be overcome, can be an advantage.
You can help others by showing why such experiences can be
>helpful, enlightening.
And your life can become fuller because you made these
>discoveries and often can value them in a way the much
>younger person never could.

04/03/13

Residents

I now understand.
I really understand.
There are events, incidents, horrors that take up permanent
    residence in my brain.
I say permanent because some have lodged here more than half a
    century.
I do not choose them; I do not invite them. Most I do not want.
Yet they come; they stay.
They interrupt me anytime they choose. morning, noon, night, early,
    late.
 They don't care what I'm doing: dining, shopping, reading, writing,
    visiting, worshipping, swimming, playing, sleeping, teaching.
They don't care where I travel: home, church, gym, the theater.
They ignore my mood: happy, sad, baffled, wounded, uncomfortable.
They're always traveling with me.
Some came all the way from Louisiana to Seattle.
They fly free to New York whenever I go.
They actually went around the world with me!
They don't always crash my present; sometimes they creep upon me.

I thought recognizing them would make them depart or, at least, lie
    dormant.
But I was wrong.
Ridding my brain of memories of injustice in the form of segregation,
    inequity, discrimination, abuse, murder is impossible.
I understand.

What saves me, though, is other residents in the form of good
      memories in my brain.
I've been blessed to have many good memories, and they too often
      show up, but always welcome, at my beck and call.

12/10/14

Understanding

Nobody is understood!
Hyperbole if ever there was one!

Nobody is COMPLETELY understood!
Reality here.

Casting aside might, the wise
        know what big or little we
        accomplish is the result of
        someone understanding
        something of someone.

12/16/13

No Thing

"Nothing" is a word I hate!
Sometimes when I hear "nothing" I know something.
The something may be wrong.
But nothing is a cover.
Nothing is not the truth, the whole truth.
Something is wanted, or something is not wanted.
I could be wrong on all counts and still nothing means
      something.
But the speaker, for whatever reason or reasons, refuses to
      elaborate, says only "nothing."

Nothing covers more territory than anyone can imagine.
Sometimes I accept nothing, no questions asked.
Sometimes I know there is something but leave the something
      alone.
Too often I'm in trouble because I take a nothing to mean
      nothing.
Other times I'm in trouble because I take a nothing to
      mean something.
And, of course, there are times I think nothing means something it
      does not mean!

Then one day I realized perhaps the answer really is nothing, no
      thing.
Perhaps the nothing is a place or a person the speaker
      wants/needs but for whatever reason or reasons chooses
      not to reveal.

And, listener, I could be in trouble forever… all because of
      no thing.

10/22/13

The Feeling of Fatigue

Some people say every racial group in the minority
        has this feeling, this uneasiness.
There is no name for it, yet there are those among us
        who know exactly this feeling.
I know they know.
Sometimes we discuss it; other times we don't.
We know it is present though there's no meter to
        measure it—unless you consider early death.
I do know that when a crime happens there are black
        people who say, "I hope nobody black did it."
(I see now some in the Muslim population say, "I hope a Muslim
        did not do this.")
Was there one white person who felt ashamed of
        what Nixon and his cohorts did? McVeigh? Bush?
Did any say, "I wish he were not white: I'm sorry for whites."

Too many of us take up burdens not ours or have burdens thrust upon us.
When the innocent culprit has been described as "dark" or
        "black," we know all the males have to be careful, more
        careful.
With all the men on edge, all of the women accustomed to being
        on edge—is it my son, brother, husband, nephew, grandchild,
        godchild?
The children suffer.
The anxiety, the frustration, the anger total a weight
        for which we have no name.

But if we live, the most obvious result is the ever-present fatigue,
    fatigue that prevents many from fulfilling potential,
    fatigue that robs humanity of we know not what.

04/16/13

Filtering

Filter, filtered, filtering, always filtering.
Life is a filter.
Whether we filter a little or a lot, with the few or the
    many, we filter, sometimes consciously, other
    times unconsciously.
Consider race, color, ethnicity, gender, birth order,
    background, politics, religion, education, sexual orientation,
    geographical origin, skin, creed, speech, nationality, vision,
    voice, ability, capability, behavior, accent, dress, appearance
    (hair, teeth, height, weight, cleanliness, neatness, piercings)
    and all the other countless ways we distinguish by separating,
    discriminating, and elevating.
    (Try listing all the ways you know.)

We can never filter completely all our conversations
    nor certainly our thoughts, but some of us know sanity negates much
    of the filtering.
Luckily, there are those who try to limit the filtering.
Sanity demands reducing filtering be the case.
Because of this reduction, "civil" remains in and expands
    civilization!

04/02/13

Teeth

Perfect teeth
Yellow teeth
Stained teeth
Rotten teeth
Missing teeth
Crooked teeth
Gaps
Gold teeth
Silver teeth
Bridges
Crowns

False teeth
Grilles

Did you know there are so many ways to describe teeth?
Are you surprised?
Can you add more ways?

Worse is not knowing who or when you are being judged
        because of one or more of the descriptions.
Worst is not knowing what you gained or lost because of your
        teeth.

04/13/13

Confronting Racists

In the process of confronting a racist, you may have to
    respond to these comments:

You don't have a sense of humor.
You're too sensitive.
You take things too personally.
You misunderstood.

But first, though racism abounds, you have to understand, in
    America, nobody is a racist.

Regardless of what is said or done, nobody is a racist.

If you can get beyond the above comments, you may confront a
    racist and open eyes and ears in the process.

12/03/12

A Way

He loved her in his own way.
That's good.
That's really good.
She was glad.
After all, she knew persons who had never been loved.
She had learned well to be grateful for any kindness.
But, she lamented, too late she learned he did not love her in her
        way, as she needed and wanted to be loved.
A not-always-obvious void was always present.
How could a void exist when she had never had what she said
        was missing?
Maybe the void of the missing piece is part of the human
        condition.
Just know the void exists.
Maybe this is the origin of love the one you're with.
Never ignoring her blessings and always grateful, she could not
        help wondering what life would have been if she had been loved in
        her way.
She never relinquished the existence of the way of being loved as
        one needs and wants to be loved.
Nor did she ever forget the more blessed are those whose ways are
        similar; a way is the way.

04/01/13

Real Peace

Real peace means no war, of course.
But real peace demands so much more
      than no war, though no war is an excellent beginning.
Peace requires no fear of war; the physical body must be safe.
There is more than adequate food, shelter, attire.
And there is no worry that any one—not to mention all three—will
      disappear.
This physical body gets preventive medical and
      dental care and treatment when needed.
And there is no worry that benefits will
      be reduced or exhausted nor service denied.
The mental body must be at least equally safe; some argue safer.
Peace provides space for education,
      a good, solid education full of knowledgeable teachers who
      recognize the humanity of all and do not see differences as
      inferiority.
Questioning without fear of repercussion is ever the case.
Peace also allows spiritual development of any and every variety.
Again there is no fear.
The stress created by the lack of any one of the above can shatter
      peace, overtly or maybe covertly, but shatter peace nevertheless.
And all of us are not always like the oyster; stress does not always
      result in our creating pearls though this stress may indeed
      make us shells of ourselves.
Finally, real peace allows us to pursue happiness as we see fit
      when that pursuit harms no one.

Opportunity and justice permeate this paradise.
The ever-present governor without exception recognizes that no
    pursuit of the ultimate personhood and real peace diminishes
    another, the other included.

2012

The Best Teachers

The best teachers know their subjects, love their subjects, and
        share their knowledge and skills.
They accept students where they are and then labor to get them
        where they ought to be, as often as possible demonstrating
        the need to rise, often exceeding any and all job requirements.
They expose.
They open doors.
They lead or direct or follow—whatever is necessary.
They want students to go farther than they themselves have gone.
And they want students to see the value of doing so.
The best teachers are not immune to pampering or pushing
        students—whatever works to bring out the best.
But the best teachers know how, when, and to what degree to
        pamper or push.
They are like birds that push their frightened babies off cliffs
        because parent birds know the babies can fly.
And they want all of their students to soar, all of them.

Dedicated to Dr. Huel D. Perkins 12/27/24 – 4/15/13
Southern University Music and Humanities Professor   *04/23/13*

Where I Sit and Stand

I do not want to sit in your seat.
Nor do I wish to fill your shoes.
I do not want to tell your story.

I don't doubt your story contains triumphs and failures.
I hope you get to tell your triumphs and failures your way, if
    you choose.

I will fill my seat and shoes, continue my story.

I would love to erase my failures.
But I do not wish to give up my triumphs.
And somehow, so often, the failures and triumphs are
    intertwined whether we sit or stand.

06/03/13

What Some Mothers Teach

For most of us, mothers are our first teachers.
They teach us prayers, for grace and night.
They teach us hygiene.
They teach us our ABC's.
They teach us to count.
They teach us our first games.
They teach us manners.
Decades later, often long after our mothers are no more, we
    remember with perfect accuracy and can perfectly do
    what mothers taught us.

06/05/12

The Haul

It's been a long haul.
I fell, had many a near fall
Supported, been supported
Rejected, been rejected
Understood, been misunderstood
Know I was carried, not how long nor how often
Lost bouts with God
Learned some whys, gave up on others
Continue to long to have a few others explained.

But overall, overall, it's been a good ride.

09/16/14

In the Same Situation

Standing up for myself says I am bold to some and
    foolish to others.
Walking away says I am brave to some and a coward
    to others.
Remaining in a situation says I am strong to some
    and weak to others.
Forgiving someone says I am wise to some and dumb to others.
Taking a friend's side in an argument says I am a
    friend to some and an intruder to others.

Try as I might, I can think of nothing that has one vantage point
    only.
Though a dilemma may appear to be the case, experience tells me
    rare are the situations in which there are two choices only.
There are often countless points between one extreme and the
    other.
So, despite the supporters and opponents, I am the one to decide.
Sometimes I can and will explain; other times I won't or can't
    explain.
This I know: the serenity that comes after the choice
    is my best evidence of having chosen correctly.

10/04/12

The Stress

Oh, the weight, the weight…

Stress is everywhere.
Stress makes babies cry: hungry, wet, uncomfortable, wanting to
 be held.
Parents' actions—or inactions—can generate stress.
Another sibling can generate stress.
Other family members can do the same.
Stress can come from the significant one in our lives.
The introduction of others can cause stress.
Some friends can fill lives with stress—no comment on enemies.
How we believe/perceive the world sees us can be stressful.
School—during any age—can envelop us in stress.
Dating—or not—can generate stress.
Being married or single can generate more stress.
Work is often full of stress: getting the job, keeping the job
 being promoted—or not—questioning our place in the world.
Shame or pride leaves a mark. Stay on the bottom or top?
 Maintain?
Health—will it worsen? How?
Will we suffer? What will the suffering be, be like? How long?
Is it mental or physical? Both?
What will the end be? Where? Status?
Will we be alone or surrounded by family and friends?

Despite what physicians say about diet and exercise,
 experience has convinced me that stress may be
 a far more significant factor in our demise than
 anyone cares to admit or can know.

06/21/12

Head, Heart, Gut

Head = Logic
Heart = Emotion
Gut = Instinct

Head, Heart, and Gut—all important for different reasons, all necessary for different reasons

How wonderful it would be to have all three agree!
Seldom is the case.
Great stories portray conflicts between any two and among the three.
Head is not always right, overrated say some.
And all the logic in all the world sometimes fails to overrule Heart.
Heart has damaged or destroyed more than anyone can measure.
Gut does not win every battle yet butts in often.

Head, Heart, and Gut—all important for different reasons, all necessary for different reasons.

Very blessed are those who regularly get the three to agree.

02/01/13

Heaven

Ages ago, I concluded, if there is a heaven, then all of us will get
    there.
There are too many undeserved hurts—small,
    medium, large, and all sizes in between.
There are too many gaps, spaces, many over which
    we have no or very little control.
A truth honestly given, often requested, becomes a
    declared war when we did not know there was a fight.
A short word emerges from a short word given, not
    necessarily by the person spoken to.
Something so trivial to one but mammoth to another creates a
    hurdle we can't leap.
The same is true of a mean deed.
These aberrations doom and damn.
We are always traveling without all the necessities—visible and
    invisible, shared and never shared.
We are always watched by those who
    care and those who don't, disappointing some
    and encouraging others with the same act.
We are always being judged by those
    who know and those who don't—failing without knowing the
    assignment or that the assignment is ours.
The betrayals, small and large
The failures, small and large
The disappointments, small and large
The uncertainties, small and large
The secrets, small and large
Alas!

Preoccupations of every kind overwhelm us as
>   attempts are made to fulfill obligations and responsibilities, some of
>   which we know others thrust upon us, often without our permission
>   or knowledge.

Someone has to know.
Only God could know everything about everything.
And by the time the handicaps of each of us is put beside our
>   wrongs, a balance is the result.

I believe there's a heaven and we'll all get there!

08/18/12

Hell

One day after yet one more terrible example of man's inhumanity
    to man, I concluded there must be Hell.
Some people have to go there; they have to!
How can you rape a baby?
How can you rape anyone?
How can you kill a child? Children?
How can you kill seventy-seven children and regret only that you
    did not kill more children?
How can you bomb a building knowing you will hurt people,
    babies even, babies who could not have known your problem
    and couldn't possibly have caused it?
How could you gas people?
How can you shoot students who want only to make life better?
Is everybody mentally deficient?

I'll stop the questions.
Just know that Hell exists, and some folks are going there.

08/23/12

One Day

One day Mondale's Comprehensive Child
    Development Act of 1971 will become law as it could have had not
    President Richard Nixon vetoed it.
One day some of the Republican luminaries who
    gathered to defeat President Barack Obama on Inauguration Day will
    apologize.
One day some of the Congresspersons who slowed or
    stymied progressive agendas will apologize.
One day citizens will marvel that we had a Supreme
    Court justice who said racial equality is racial
    entitlement.

I say this because I know of and know many
    persons who cringe at the horror of slavery, the
    ignorance of segregation, the meanness of
    discrimination.
I say this because I know of and know many persons
    who wonder that laws could and did say first people in a land could
    be driven to reservations; Africans could be abducted from their lands
    and could not be citizens in "The New World"; a man could be 3/5 of
    a person; human beings could be slaves; women could not vote.
I know because I am in that group who wonder at all
    of the inanities and inequities perpetuated because of race, gender,
    sex—characteristics not ordained by choice.

One day the latest inanities and inequities will be the
    subject of equally amazing gazes, ahs, and how-could-
    theys.

Knowing this one day is approaching prevents me
> from exploding and imploding today, daily gives me hope.

I have but patiently to continue my journey,
> willingly, regularly pointing out the asininity of
> the past and how today we have to do better, be
> better, or, at the least, I myself have to do and be better.

01/25 & 03/05/13

Confessions

"I'm not who I was," said the father who had been absent for decades.
"Neither am I," said the used-to-be-child with his best possible response.
Whatever the reason, nobody is the same.
Nothing alive remains the same.
We must stop thinking we can absent ourselves, return at
> will or when we are "up to it," and expect everything to
> restart or continue as if little or nothing bad happened.

Neither apologies nor sincerity banish pain or negate time.
People are not pots that can be set on the back burner to
> "simmer" or "warm."

We must stop believing all is well because we are now ready
> to be responsible.

We must stop thinking being ready can diminish or erase the
> experiences or lack thereof.

Somehow we must do and be better earlier rather than late.
We must stop saying "better late than never" and realize "better
> never late" is more apt.

We must consider possible repercussions prior to actions:
> sex, parenting, smoking, drugs, alcohol, education, saving,
> etc.

03/08/15

A Brief History

When I was a little girl, I had lots of hope.
I remember.
I was convinced that by the time my friends and I grew up
    there would be no segregation, no discrimination.
Old people were responsible, I reasoned.
They would be dead by the time I grew up.
Then Emmett Till came.
I saw the picture of his body in the casket.
I wondered how anyone could do that kind of damage to any body.
Emmett Till was always a person to me, a boy just a few years older than I.
Late that same year Rosa Parks refused to give up her seat.
My hope portion grew.
The March on Washington came.
Angry my mom would not let me go, I sat close to the seventeen-inch black
    and white television watching every move.
Then came the bombing of a church the next month.
How can a person bomb a church?
And then to learn a group of persons bombed a church!
Would not one person think this an awful deed and halt it?
Between '64 and '65 my hope went from mountaintop to valley—
    Voting Rights Act to deaths of Goodman, Schwerner, and Cheney;
    Selma March I and Selma March II.
Fifty years and a graph of my hope mimics a not-too-high
    mountain range.
There were horrible rulings by the Supreme Court before
    my time: Plessy vs. Ferguson, Dred Scott Decision,
    Separate but Equal, to name major violations.

I had come to believe the federal government was better, would
        rectify wrongs, protect the innocent, punish the guilty.

But too often laws touting fairness in voting, education, housing, and
        employment were made but not enforced; maybe they
        are not and never were enforceable.

All I know is that I myself am most likely put in that category of old people and there's probably a little girl with lots of hope and I hate to think that her hope, despite the efforts, lives, and deaths of many, will be eroded as mine has been.

03/10/15

My Craziness

The craziness in me is gone.
There never was much, but that little had to go.
That ubiquitous they
>	beat it out of me
>	cut it out of me
>	shot it out of me
>	bombed it out of me.

So, I have to be sane.
There is neither time nor space for Craziness.
Craziness never pauses nor sleeps.

So I've been drafted into the small militia.
I've only one option.

Sane wailers must speak now, act now, warn now.
Sanity can win, but not easily and not cheaply, not permanently.
Sanity must lead, overthrow if necessary.
Sanity gets no break, cannot rest; the dunces are ever-ready.
Only Sanity can wipe out Craziness—and wipe it out repeatedly
>	before Craziness maims and kills all of us.

07/24/12

A Mind of Its Own

My consciousness has a mind of its own.
I say what I will not think about, yet my
    consciousness often takes over.

For instance, I love the Blue Angels despite the
    energy use, noise pollution, traffic snarls,
    crowd attraction, scared beings, unfair
    recruitment, and old-fashioned imperialism.

But I never see the Blue Angels without thinking about
    Bigger Thomas.
You know Bigger; don't you?

A creation of Richard Wright, Bigger says, "Those white boys sure can fly" as he's walking down the street and planes streak over his head. When he makes the statement, perhaps he has no idea one could take it so many ways.

For me, the white boys can fly over the fictitious Bigger—and the
    real me—in countless ways, still. And do.

Take another example: I drink from a water fountain. I want only a cold drink, but two, maybe three out of ten times, I am reminded of colored and white signs including times even when I am in a place overwhelmingly filled with black people.

Or, I get on a bus, another rare occurrence. And more than one-half century after learning I had to sit in the back of the bus, I remember the eleven-year old me who learned I could not sit in the front.

And there were my teachers being forced to buy an outfit and take it home to try it on. (I don't think I ever had anything from The Palace, Monroe, Louisiana's most exclusive store.) If for some reason the garment was not satisfactory, they had to trek back to the store to select another or get a refund. I wonder how often someone kept something because returning it was such a strain in more ways than one.

Still another example: Seldom do I use a public restroom; however, my mind recalls all those years of not being allowed to use any public restroom other than the one designated in all downtown. Montgomery Ward's will always be on a pedestal for me although somewhere along the way I began wondering if maybe Ward's "won" the lottery and was forced to let "coloreds" use their restrooms.

Sitting in the balcony in a theater, entering the front door of a doctor's office, dining at any restaurant I choose, having a photo taken, visiting the library, sitting in a courtroom.... The list of what was colored and white, the governing rules, and why could be longer. I'm trying to wrest my mind from thoughts of what happened long ago, trying to eradicate memories that remind me of the day my consciousness became aware....

Seafair Day Seattle 08/05/12

Silent Dolls

When Shel was nine, she did not want to be ten,
Said she feared her dolls would soon stop talking to her.
And she was right.
Many adults could have told her she was right, but she
       figured it out for herself.
The kindest adults did not want to tell her.
The longer she lived, the less she heard the sweet, soothing
       agreeable sounds of peace coming from the dolls.
And though she can't recall the exact date, the talk of the
       dolls did cease.

The voices of the dolls stopped—replaced by noise,
       noise which got louder and louder, often inaudible.
When the adult Shel heard, she heard different words.
Instead of Harmony, she heard Cacophony.
In truth, demands ruled: discord often overruled.
Compromise was the order of the day, trust never a guarantee.
Nothing was done or given freely.
So often, good words were said but not always meant.
She learned I love you really meant I love you if….I love you
       when….I love you as long as…I love you, but…
She learned I'll take care of you meant I'll take care of you
       if…I'll take care of you when….I'll take care of you as long
       as…, I'll take care of you, but ….
I'll support you was followed by the same qualifiers.
When she uttered, "I don't want to be ten; the dolls will soon stop
       talking to me," all of those years ago she had been right.

What saved her was the memory of all those times the dolls talked. She couldn't have known how much the doll talk prepared her for life after the dolls became silent.

02/13/05

The Deed

$5,000,000 settlement.

That's what the judge said.

But no amount of money can make this
        deed right.

No "I never intended."

No "I'm sorry."

No "I accept responsibility."

No "I made a mistake."

Seriously, the perpetrator probably cared not
        that his deed was unacceptable, intolerable, not a viable
        option, and not in his backyard.

The deed may as well be acceptable, tolerated, an option.

The deed was definitely not in his backyard.

Of the many consequences, the worst is realizing nothing,
        absolutely nothing can restore life to what it was before
        the deed.

03/27/12

Two of Me

It's a full-time job just being me!
Taking care of myself takes more time than I have!
Perhaps two of me could solve my problems.
I could read; the other me could clean the closet.
I could write; the other me could fold and store laundry.
I could see one play; the other me could see a baseball game.
I could visit a sick friend; the other me could visit the friend in hospice.
I could teach children; the other me could teach adults.
I could read; the other me could load or unload the dishwasher.
I could vacuum; the other me could dust.

But, there's only one of me.
And I have to do all of the above and more.
Answer: I have to work as if there are two or three of me.

05/10/12

"Obama Wins"
(A Senior Black Woman Reads the Newspaper the Day After Barack H. Obama Is Elected President)

Only black folks of a certain age and
    background know the true
    meaning of *The Mississippi Times*
    headline "President Obama Wins."
Maybe President Obama himself is
    too young to realize the true
    meaning of his win.

The reader, however, knows her joy
    cannot erase the possibility of
    his being harmed.
There's no post-racial USA, may never be.
Too many of us are too far from judging
    each other by the content of our
    character.
The reader's face shows her awareness.
Though she could not be certain
    what would happen, she knew
    President Obama's path would not be easy.
No one ever could have guessed nor will ever
    know how many folks failed to
    vote for President Obama because of his
    blackness.
For many, his qualifications mean
    nothing regardless of the
    qualifications of previous
    presidents.

Affirmative action is evil, they say, and
    every non-white person not an
    entertainer or athlete has succeeded
    only because of affirmative action.
Grades mean nothing.
Honors and accolades are dismissed.

He's had to deal with the so-called
    birthers. (If they thought for a
    minute, they would know John
    McCain and Hillary Clinton
    checked this early in the
    contest.)

A finger in anyone's face is a universal insult, but the face of the
    President of the United States? On camera?
Will the speaker refuse the first black President's request to
    speak to Congress?

Maybe someone will call the
    President a liar—during an
    address to Congress.
Will there be signs attacking his
    ethnicity rather than his policies?

Could some Congress persons
        refuse to raise the debt ceiling
        though it means lowering the
        country's credit standing?
What if the Senate minority leader
        declares "My top political
        priority over the next two years
        should be to deny President
        Obama a second term?"

The reader would like to be his
        catcher in the rye, but she knows
        no one can protect any of us all of the time,
        the President included.
All she can do is temper her celebration.
She has moved from praying and
        hoping and wishing he would
        be safe and win to praying and hoping and
        wishing he'll be safe and succeed.
But always, always does she know
        the Confederacy is alive in the
        hearts and minds of many in
        Mississippi and the other forty-nine
        states.
The battle continues to rage and,
        unfortunately, may never die.

The reader is not alone in knowing
        this fact as certainly as the
        perpetrators are of continuing
        the war.
Her look will almost always be neither
        happy nor sad but hesitant as she
        simultaneously wishes this bold man
        well and safe.

09/12, 16/12　　　　Inspired by Chaz Lindsey's painting of the same name

Why We Fall in Love

Did we fall in love because of
- the uniform?
- the height?
- the weight?
- the teeth?
- the body?
- the hair?
- the color?
- the race?
- the speech?
- the shape?
- the vocabulary?
- the status?
- the class?
- the money?

You may have been attracted by any one of the above, but rarely is any one of the above enough to sustain what the wise—and not-so-wise—call love.

05/05/12

A Family

Dad says Mom and children are crazy.
Mom says Dad and children are crazy.
One sibling says Mom, Dad, and other siblings are crazy.
And so say the other siblings at various times, never in the
        company of family.
No reply from the listener was uttered, maybe not expected.
But the listener felt certain that members of the family were not
        alone in their assessments of each family member.

05/17/13

Staying

I stayed.
Often I did not want to stay.
Often I did not think I could stay.
So many told me not to stay.
Logic definitely said don't stay.

Didn't think I could stay.
Didn't think I should stay.
Never knew I would stay.

But stay I did.

2012

Waiting

Dressed in her Sunday best from modest hat to
    sensible shoes,
Just a tiny bit of her pretty slip showing—you know,
    just enough to make someone say how pretty it is.
Little old lady is waiting on the front porch, in a
    wheelchair.
She looked calm, rather pleasant.
Only God knew her rejoicing in this day was difficult.
But she had never doubted His goodness, knowing
    early He was good all the time.
Believer that she was and continues to be, she waited, one
    suitcase by her side, remembering her long history in
    the house: the long ago time the healthy she and her beloved
    late husband had purchased it, their biggest expense ever;
    getting ready for the first baby, baby's arrival; the easier time of preparing
    for second baby, baby's arrival; recognizing,
    acknowledging the authorities they were for the third baby,
    baby's arrival; being the center for the neighborhood
    children, church folks, reunions—actually anyone who might
    show up; watching the children—theirs and others'—
    growing from toddlers to teen-agers, in junior high, high
    school, playing, sports, dating; getting ready for the weddings.
Her mind was flooded with memory after memory, far
    more good than bad.
She would have to leave her beloved sanctuary.
Yet she smiled as she came back to today, continued her
    waiting.

Time and money were removing her from the
>premises.
But no destination nor "for sale" sign could ever
>deprive her of her real treasures.

09/15/12   Inspired by Chaz Lindsey's painting of the same name

Selling

Selling a poem, a song, music, a photograph, or a newspaper, a
        story, a book, or a business
Selling clothes or stocks or cars
Selling a talent or a service
This common thread of selling is not always obvious.

But the sellers, like Willy Loman, are
        "way out there in the blue riding a smile and a shoestring."

What can be baffling, overwhelming is the greatest sale: realizing
        that so often we ourselves must similarly sell ourselves!

08/12

Definitely Ill

Of course, the pilot was ill.
Only an ill person would kill himself.
And to kill others, others who had nothing to do with his
    illness is more evidence of his illness.
Forget the law of self-preservation.
It was not in force that day.

So he always wanted to be a pilot.
Pardon me, but what if he had lived the kind of life that
    allowed space for other careers?
What if he had other interests and hobbies?

Gratefully, most of us are not so focused on one area that
    we destroy ourselves and others if our dream in that
    area is not fulfilled or thwarted.

03/30/15

My America

No one's ever asked me about "My America."
I do have one.
I know America, have to know America.
I'm proud when I hear Canadian Robert Sinclair's
    anthem about the Americans, how we help
    everybody but no one helps us, but I know what
    Michelle Obama meant when she said "For
    the first time in my adult lifetime, I am really proud
    of my country."
I know the major role we played in World War II, but I
    know some of our worst enemies gained and
    remained in power because of our power.
I know the foreign aid we give, how we give more
    dollars than any other country, but I know we do
    not give as large a percentage of our gross
    national product as many countries.
I know about Brown vs. the Board of Education, but I
    know about Dred Scott (no one of African descent
    has the right to sue) and Plessy (separate but equal
    affirmed) and Jim Crow.
I know the people and countries we have liberated,
    but I admit we are often responsible for
    overthrowing or murdering officials as legitimately
    elected as some officials in our country.
I know how we have cleaned up many polluted sites,
    but I know how we've knowingly and recklessly polluted other sites in
    our country and the world.

I know dignitaries from all over the world come here for
> medical care, but I know the poor, especially people of color, often
> don't get necessary medical care or have passed one or two hospitals
> and died en route to the charity or colored hospital.

I know the role we've played in eliminating some of the
> world's dreaded diseases, but I know about the
> secretly performed sterilizations, Tuskegee syphilis
> experiment, and repeated robbing of Henrietta Lacks.

I know how people have risked their lives to come to
> this country and been welcomed, but many people born
> here were killed because of the color of their skin.

I know we have some of the best institutions of higher
> learning in the world, but I know how some inner
> city and rural schools are jungles.

I know some of the poorest people get the opportunity
> to go to college, but thousands more are incarcerated—
> usually poor and uneducated.

I can say God bless America, but I know why the veteran Rev. Dr.
> Jeremiah Wright could say, "God, damn America."

You get my point.

Neither time nor space permits me to name all the good and all the
> bad.

I'm still learning.

But this I know: My America has a split personality: good and bad.

So many Americans know nothing about this bad side
> or quickly say, "That was a long time ago" or, my
> favorite, "I had nothing to do with that."

America is Dr. Jekyll and Mr. Hyde, Good Witch and Bad Witch.
I love my country right or wrong.
And I'm not leaving it permanently.
But I want my country to do what's right—all the time.
And how do we know what's right?
We ask ourselves if we want to be treated as our
        country treats all of its own and some foreigners.
We don't consider what others had or did not have, know
        or did not know.
We honestly admit we would or would not want to be
        treated in the same manner.
Anytime the answer is no, we don't want to be treated
        in that manner, then we refuse to treat others in
        that manner!
My America could become the America so many had/have in
        mind, believe exists.
And God really will bless America, bless it more.

04/26/12

What Was Taken

From Africa were taken
                    Our families and homes
                    Our countries
                    Our culture
In the "New World" were taken
                    Our families
                    Our culture
                    Rights to G. I. benefits
                    Opportunity to get loans
                    Rights to music
            Access to education: laws against teaching blacks to read
                    Credit for inventions
                    Wages
                    Never granted 40 acres and a mule
Health: not just no or poor medical care but experiments to sicken and kill us,
                    sterilize us without consent.
                    Dignity.
All of the years through slavery, segregation, discrimination we worked without pay
                    or low pay.
Too many today have no work and no pay.
If only our ancestors had gotten wages….
Better, if only no one had concocted and administered that "peculiar institution,"
                    imagine.
Only God knows how many inhumane actions took place in the centuries-old deed.
Too many of us know so little or so much, and all of us suffer the results.

06/01/15

My Friends

Father/Allah protect them.
They know not what they do.
They are two of the nicest, gentlest men I have ever known.
But they hail from a country mention of which makes some
        Americans crazy and some crazy Americans crazier.
With their accents and one with his shoulder-length hair, they
        can be hurt by sick people.
I do not want to tell them this.
I do not want them to fear.
I want them safe without telling them they must be on guard.
I want them to see what they believe America to be.
I want them to see the best America although I know the best
        America is not always displayed.
I am not paranoid.
History has proved that sick people harm people for no reason.
These men have said little negative about America, and I have
        often agreed with them; many people won't agree.
Police may stop them; police do not always protect us; police come
        from the same pool as the general populace.
But my friends have no idea how easily they can be hurt, killed.
And all because they are not Americans.

08/25/12

Plagues

What plagues a person?

 Usually the plague is not something we talk about or reveal but something that is forever on our mind, not in the recesses but near the surface, something that annoys, preoccupies.

- Rose Kennedy couldn't forget that she was set to go to school in England, father had agreed, but when his businessmen friends learned of this, they told him he could not send his daughter abroad: sending her abroad to be educated says an American education is inferior.
- LBJ never forgot that RFK—despite brother JFK's invitation—asked LBJ three times not to run.
- Gennie, in the late stage of Alzheimer's, continued to remember that throughout her career, "They tried to take my job."
- Robin Gibb did not want the Bee Gees to be thought of as a disco group.

Nothing like the human brain, nothing.

The human brain may be the greatest proof that we are indeed made in the image of God.

05/17/13

Half Lies, Partial Truths?

I love you, but I'm not in love with you.

We can have a casual relationship; no one will get hurt.

I don't want to jump you; I want to get to know you first.

I meant I love you when I said I love you.

I want what you want.

It didn't mean anything.

I'll do anything you say.

I just want to be with you.

God sent me.

06/05/12

Half the World

The American girl learned early not to do anything
    better than boys, "boy things," that is, especially
    if she wanted his attention.
    Women often continue the charade.
The Saudi girl learned earlier still what was for boys
    and what was for girls: she serves and loves serving, it appears.
    Being one of four wives is subsequently much better—not to mention
    safer—than having a baby out of wedlock.
The English girl knows the meaning of "primogeniture."
    Kate and William will parent the first baby whose gender
    does not determine whether she gets the throne.
Half the world, they tell us; we women are half the world.
Look at the number of countries; then look at the
    number of women leaders.
One in three women around the world is physically
    and/or sexually abused, often by persons they know: dads,
    brothers, boyfriends, husbands.
Two-thirds of illiterate adults are women.
79.7% of women can read and write.
Great Britain's 58 kings and 8 queens, the U. S.'s 44 male
    presidents…
Considering we women are half the world, we have to do less
    of the menial work and more of the work of the other half, especially
    if that means reducing the violence in the world.

07/13

Police Action

"Name what comes to mind when you hear '60s," said the
    conference leader.
Shouts went out: "Civil rights," "MLK," "hippies," "Motown,"
    "assassinations," "flower power," "Viet Nam," "Viet Nam
    War."
Depending on your social location, the answers vary.
Then we forgot about it.
The next day, however, we were told there was an announcement.
A female—Viet Nam veteran, we later learned—told us there was
    no war in Viet Nam, made clear that what we had in Viet Nam was a
    "police action."
The group was quiet, quiet.
No one booed or shouted or said right on.

But after the meeting, anyone who mentioned it—and many did—said, "It
    was a war."
What I remember is 58,000 Americans killed and unknown
    thousands more from other countries killed, especially North
    and South Viet Nam.
And there are the uncounted physically and mentally injured, the
    ones at home, the ones whose illnesses appeared after being
    discharged, the damaged offspring.
I rarely speak the name, but whenever I read of a Viet Nam vet
    killing and/or being killed, I wonder for a moment how different life
    would have been had there been no Viet Nam in his life.
Knowing that the majority of vets have no such ends is no comfort; I am glad
    their lives did not end permanently, of course.
Police action.
Yes. OK.
You'll get no war of words from me.

08/10/13

Views from An Axe and a Tree

"Get over it!" said to an African American about Slavery

"It's in the past!" said to a survivor of the Holocaust

"Let's move forward," said to a Japanese born in an internment camp

"Get on with your life," said to rape and molestation victims

Move the statements around.
Any one admonition can, could, does go with any statement.
Comments said cavalierly, often sincerely, are said only by
       those or descendants of those who clearly have not suffered the "it"
       that prompted the advice.
Healthy or not, the Shona proverb is correct: what the axe
       soon forgets, the tree—or stump—long remembers.

12/10/14

A New Revelation

I know God.
He is omnipotent.
He is omnipresent.
He is omniscient.

Omniscience fascinates me most.
He knows everything.
He knows everything about everything.
I should put a period there.
But being far from omniscient, I sometimes question His
    omniscience regarding me.
I know that upsets some folks.
It upsets me.
But when I'm told He knows how much I can bear and I'm
    weighed down, I question.

Then, sometime after, it occurs to me.
I overcame.
I'm still here.
I'm still telling the story.
So I have to rethink.

Here is my new conclusion: God has more faith in me than
    I have in myself, much more.

06/03/15

Good Tireds

The day I traipsed around the Acropolis wishing the caryatids were there but elated I could see them in the nearby museum

The day I decided to go to New York every year, at least once, visiting and revisiting museums and parks, seeing and re-seeing plays

The days I trudged to the top of Diamond Head, St. Peter's, the Pont Du Gard

The days I saw two plays, *Macbeth* and *A Man for All Seasons*, for example

The day I saw classmates from one-half a century ago

The day I swam the width of the pool; the day I swam a mile

The days I have the nieces and nephews and now the grandnieces and grandnephews all to myself and let them choose what we do and how long we stay

Each day I was exhausted, exhausted, exhausted.
But I was grateful, grateful, grateful.
All days ended with me being tired, but the tired was good.

In each instance my one regret was not always sharing the experience with others who would have loved it as I did.

11/08/13

Perils of Their Way

Let them do it their way.
They can do it their way.
No argument?
I differ.
I say, perhaps, maybe, yes, on occasion.

What's their way?

Do they let dogs run loose?
Do they bully?
Do they give children drugs?
Do they fail to secure guns?
Do they text while driving?
Do they drive while drunk?

How many folks are doomed because they did whatever "their way"?
What if someone had told them the hazards of their way?
What if someone had encouraged them to act in another
    way?

Sure, let them do it their way but not when we know their
    way is harmful.
And there are times when some folks know a way is terrible.
Too often the uninvolved suffer as others do something "their
    way."

So many tragedies happen in an instant.
We must stop being quiet when being quiet means harm or
    death to the actors and or those around them.

03/15/15

Police at Work

139 rounds spent
13 officers fired shots
49 rounds
1 officer fired 49 rounds
15 rounds—fired standing on top of the hood of the car
15 rounds into two persons sitting in the front seat
2 unarmed persons

Add the numbers.
Here is the total, bottom line, as it really was:
Judge says homicide justified.
Car backfired.
These police don't know backfiring from gunshots.
These police didn't know car occupants were unarmed.
These police were protecting themselves.
These police were afraid for their lives.
These police were protecting the public.
The public is in trouble—or some of the public is in
      trouble.

05/25/15

Thankful

Thankful more folks than ever before—not everyone unfortunately—understand what racism is

Thankful that among this group are siblings, grandparents, aunts and uncles who will do anything to protect their loved ones—including calling people on their language and actions

Thankful that more folk than ever before are working to erase isms of every kind

Thankful I can see changes, significant changes

Thankful I am here at this time where I can contribute to the change

Yes, I have many reasons to be thankful not at Thanksgiving only but every day all through the day.

And I am thankful.

Thankful, thankful, thankful.

11/10/13

INDEX

Accepted Silences	57
Afraid for My Life I	53
Afraid for My Life II	54
Afraid for My Life III	56
An American Exercise	16
Ask Questions Later	45
Aware	86
Being Myself	82
Benefits of Reading	87
The Best Teachers	118
Black All of Her Life	35
A Brief History	130
Can't Forget; Forgive	144
Care	1
The Change	31
Charades and Masquerades	28
A Child and an Adult Watch TV	10
Complete	11
Confessions	129
Confronting Racists	114
Cry	73
The Deed	137
Definitely Ill	148

167

Disadvantages Overcome	105
The Discomfort of Relativity	39
Diversity	96
The Emperor	33
Explanations	15
Failing Memory	2
A Family	144
The Feeling of Fatigue	110
Filtering	112
Flash: Breaking News	44
The Footsteps	26
Good Tireds	160
Grim Reaper	47
Half the World	156
Half Lies, Partial Truths	156
The Haul	129
Head, Heart, Gut	123
Heaven	124
Hell	126
His Final Act for Her	7
His Ways	101
In an Instant	99
In the Same Situation	121

Justice	46
Knowing	34
Kudos to the Pope	103
Late and Future Apologies	12
Little You and Big I	52
Losses	64
Loving Couples	77
Merging of Mom and Me	79
Michelangelo	103
A Mind of Its Own	133
Mr. Right	58
My America	149
My Craziness	132
My Friends	153
My Mantra	84
The Need for Money	91
A New Revelation	159
News	49
No Thing	109
Non-Fiction Please	63
Not Having Your Way	89
Nothing Goes Away	83
"Obama Wins"	139

Occupy	60
One Day	127
Past, Present, and Future	88
Perils of Their Way	161
Plagues	154
Police Action	157
Police at Work	162
Puzzle Solved	92
Questions for God	5
A Random Move	4
Real Peace	116
Refugees	32
Repercussions	76
Re-Register with The Rabbi	62
Residents	106
Responses	95
Selling	147
Shootings	21
Silent Dolls	135
Sitting and Standing	41
Six and Sixty	59
Somebody	74
Sometimes I Can't	20

Speaking of the Emperor	33
Staying	144
The Stress	122
Stuck	66
Suggestions	42
Teeth	113
The Throw-Away People	78
Trauma	93
Trees and Forests	3
Trust God	51
Two of Me	138
Two Pictures	9
Unwanted Love	25
Uppermost	65
Validation Needs	25
Value of a Study	104
Views from an Axe and a Tree	158
Waiting	145
A Way	115
What Am I to Do?	1
What I Hear	40
What Some Mothers Teach	120
What Was Taken	152

What We Want	44
Where I Sit and Stand	119
Where Is George Bush?	14
Where to Wash	44
Why Not?	6
Why They Don't Tell	102
Why We Fall in Love	143
Wondering vs. Knowing	98
Your Pool	75
Your Standard	43

About the Author

GEORGIA STEWART MCDADE, a Louisiana native who has lived in Seattle more than half her life, loves reading and writing. As a youngster she wrote and produced plays for her siblings and neighbors and collaborated with church youth to write plays for special occasions. Earning a Bachelor of Arts from Southern University, Master of Arts from Atlanta University, and Ph. D. from University of Washington, the English major spent more than thirty years teaching at Tacoma Community College but also found time to teach at Seattle Community College, Seattle University, the University of Washington, Lakeside School, Renton Technical College, and Zion Preparatory Academy. As a charter member of the African-American Writers' Alliance (AAWA), McDade began reading her stories in public in 1991. She credits AAWA with making her regularly write poetry. It was with this group she began reading her poetry in public. For a number of years she has written poems inspired by art at such sites as Gallery 110, Seattle Art Museum, Columbia City Gallery, and Onyx Fine Arts Collective. For several years she wrote for Pacific Newspapers, especially the *South District Journal*. Convinced all of us can learn to write well, McDade conducts and participates in a variety of writing workshops. "Good writing can force us to think and think critically; we can theorize, organize, analyze, and synthesize better," says she. She has edited several books. A prolific writer, she has works in AAWA anthologies *I Wonder as I Wander*, *Gifted Voices*, *Words? Words! Words*, and *Threads*. Her works include *Travel Tips for Dream Trips*, questions and answers about her six-month, solo trip around the world; *Outside the Cave* (2009) and *Outside the Cave II* (2012), collections of poetry; and numerous essays, stories, and poems. Among her several writing projects are two biographies, a collection of stories, and journals kept during her travels.

www.ingramcontent.com/pod-product-compliance
Lightning Source LLC
Chambersburg PA
CBHW051946290426
44110CB00015B/2132